THE GOD OF MY MAN OF GOD:

The Spirit Behind The Mantle!

CHIOMA AFOKE

authorHOUSE

AuthorHouse™
1663 Liberty Drive
Bloomington, IN 47403
www.authorhouse.com
Phone: 833-262-8899

Published by AuthorHouse 01/25/2022

ISBN: 978-1-6655-4941-7 (sc)
ISBN: 978-1-6655-4940-0 (e)

Library of Congress Control Number: 2022901054

CONTENTS

CHAPTER ONE

MINISTERS: UNTO GOD

Serving the God that you do not Know

THERE ARE MANY WHO ARE walking around today, innocently believing that they Know God, but they are far from knowing God. Knowing God comes with a level of information, experience and understanding of the person of the Holy Spirit. It is the person of the Holy Spirit that introduces God to you in form of convictions, and to progress to knowing God, you will also need the person of the Holy Spirit. There is no level of progression in the things of God, especially in knowing God without an experience of the person of the Holy Spirit. He introduces you to the different levels in God.

There are many men of God who are serving God, but do not know him. It is a very dangerous thing to go on serving God that you do not know and have not experienced.

Let us look at the book of 1 Samuel 3:1, hear what the Bible said here about Samuel who ministered unto the LORD before Eli. The word ministered here is a Hebrew root word "Sharath" (Shaw-rath), a word which means to render a service as a servant. This means, Samuel was a servant and a minister of the things of God in the temple. The bible also made it clear that the word of God was precious in those days, because God didn't really speak much, and there was nothing like open visions.

Now when you look at 1Samuel 3:7, the Bible made it clear that Samuel did not yet know the LORD and had not experienced the word of the LORD. In other words, Samuel was a minister who served GOD in the presence of the priest Eli, but he did not know God, neither had he experienced the word of the LORD.

The word "know" used here is the Hebrew word "YADA" which means a knowledge that is experiential, observational or by acquaintance. A personal knowledge of someone through an experience. Samuel is said to have not experienced God nor his word, yet he was a minister unto the LORD.

Now, tell me how you can properly serve a God whose words you cannot hear, nor have experienced his person? This is a very important point, this type of service unto God, didn't happen only in the Old Testament or in the Bible, it is happening today in our world as believers of the Gospel of Jesus Christ. Many have been following routine and religious cycle of serving the Lord but have not yet known or experienced the Lord.

I tell you by experience that this was my case, I was busy following routine Christianity, I thought I knew the Lord, believe me I did. I was a born again, and was Holy Spirit filled, but I did not know the Lord by encounter or experience.

I was in a hotel room in South Africa where I went to attend an international conference in AMI (Alleluia Ministries International). After the Friday evening service, seeing the Man of God Apostle Alph Lukau manifest the presence of God, I was thrilled. That night in my hotel room, I began to pray as I was ready to go to sleep. What was my prayer?

I asked God, what is my purpose on earth? Why is the devil after me? And as I continued to ask God to help me discover my purpose on the earth, something began to happen to me.

You see people of God, this is usually the prayer point that many believers pray, believing since they are in the faith, the next thing is to get to know why they are in the world, the purpose for their existence. Believe me, as genuine as that prayer was, and as powerful as it seemed, God told me it was the wrong prayer.

That night, while I was finishing up my prayer request unto God to show me why I am here on the earth, I heard an audible voice of God, and He said to me clearly "Why not pray that you get to know me?" I was so shocked hearing this voice, but I responded immediately, I said unto God, I thought I knew you Father, I am so sorry Father. And I heard him again "When you know me, you will know yourself."

First, I was so shocked at what I was hearing, I had been born again for seventeen years as of then, and I have been involved in the things of God, been a leader in the church etc. so, this was really shocking to me. It wasn't that shocking to me that I didn't know myself, that's why I prayed that prayer in the first place, but it was shocking to hear the Lord say that I didn't know him.

This confirms what Jesus said in Mathew 7:22-23 "Many will say to Me in that Day, 'Lord, Lord, have we not prophesied in Thy name, and in Thy name have cast out devils, and in Thy name done many wonderful works?

And then I will declare to them publicly, 'I never knew you; depart from Me [you are banished from My presence], you who act wickedly [disregarding My commands]."

The worst place to find oneself, is a place where everything looks good in your own eyes, and your own standard, but to hear a different thing on the last day. Hear what Jesus said here, "you who act wickedly, disregarding my commands". His command is this "I am the way and the truth and the life. No one comes to the father except through me" (John 14:6). Many are going through many other routes and in search for God but neglecting Jesus by neglecting the Holy Spirit.

Let us consider Acts 19:1-6 when Paul the Apostle met some disciples at the Church of Ephesus, seeing the way they operated and served God, he asked a very important question, "Did you receive the Holy Spirit when you believed?" Guess what they answered? They said, "We have not even heard that there is a Holy Spirit." These men were disciples, and they did not know anything about the Holy Spirit. Yet, they were rendering services in the Church.

What I am telling you is the reason why many are failing in ministry today, because they are ministering unto God, but do not know the God they minister unto.

Trust me, by the time you discover this truth, and you get to know God by experience, your life and your work with God will take a new turn. Just like the disciples in Ephesus, Paul laid hands on them, they had an experienced with God, and they prophesied. (Acts 19:6).

That night in my hotel room, I pondered greatly at what I heard, I humbled myself, and I began to pray that prayer, "Lord teach me to know you, reveal yourself to me" I am still praying that prayer until this day. As the Lord began to answer this prayer, I realized that truly, I do not know the Lord, and it is a very dangerous thing to think you know God, when you don't.

CHAPTER TWO

THE SEVEN SPIRITS OF GOD

THERE ARE INDEED DIFFERENT LEVELS in which you can truly know God, who God is, can be known through seven different levels. Your access to information in God is determined by the place or the level you find yourself. What does this mean? I am saying that to know God, you must be exposed to the Seven Spirits of God, which are seven different lamps (light) burning before the throne of God. The information you will be able to access in life is determinant on the level of knowledge you have about God.

The seven Spirits of God which are represented by the seven lamps of fire burning before the throne in heaven (Revelation 4:5) are the eyes through which man must come to know God. This is what Apostle Paul was saying in Ephesians 1:18 "That the eyes of your understanding be enlighten…" This means, knowing God must come through the eyes of your understanding, and only the Spirit of God can open the eyes of your understanding.

As I was saying, there are seven different levels (burning lamps) through which you can know God. In other words, the knowledge of who God is, comes in seven different levels and stages. As you go from one level to another, you gain more information better and deeper than the last level. As we are seated in heavenly places in Christ Jesus (Ephesians 2:6), we are also seated on different levels and positions in God. If you are found at the seventh level or stage, you can function exactly like Jesus. This is when you can do what he did on the earth, and even greater work as he commanded us in John 14:12. You have access to the seven Spirits of God.

The first level of knowing God: The Spirit of the fear of the Lord: It is the level at which you enter the Kingdom of God. It is the Holy Spirit who convicts you of sin and ignites your heart with a holy fear, which makes you seek after God. At this level, you seek to get salvation, to give your heart to God by believing and confessing his son Jesus Christ. Here, you are at the feet of Jesus, and as you press on for further knowledge of who he is, you begin to climb the ladder.

The second level of knowing God: The Spirit of the Knowledge of God: You have just started asking questions in your heart, you are pressing further in deep thoughts. You are saying what more is there in this gift of salvation? Now that you are in the kingdom, what next? As you ask these questions, the Spirit of God begins to enlighten you and lead you through the word of God, through things, and places that will help you grow in the knowledge of God.

The third level of knowing God: The Spirit of Might of God: you are equipped in this level, because of the information you accessed in the second level. This Spirit of might comes on you to help you progress into working in the Kingdom of God. Here, you begin laboring in the Kingdom because of what you have been exposed to or what you know. Many times, pastors and people of God get stuck here, they become complaisant because of the access to this anointing called "The Spirit of Might of God". It is the power of God, an ability released to do the work of God.

The fourth level of knowing God: The Spirit of Counsel of God: this is a level of apostleship; you are given the ability to judge on matters as pertaining the kingdom of God. As an apostle, you have many sectors and people under you, and you judge on the matters concerning them. You offer them counsel, and you are a guide to those who labor in the kingdom of God.

The fifth and the sixth level of knowing God: The Spirit of Understanding and The Spirit of Wisdom of God: These are the prophetic levels. If you are in the prophetic, you would have attained the other four levels of the knowledge of God to get to the fifth and the sixth level. You cannot be a prophet and occupy the office of a prophet without these levels of the knowledge of God. The prophetic manifests a level of understanding of God, and a very high level of wisdom of God. Based on your progress in accordance with the information you gain access to on the fifth and sixth levels, you will either stay here, or be elected to the Chamber of God which is the seventh level of knowing God.

The seventh level is "The Spirit of Yahweh": This is the Holies of Holy, the boardroom of Almighty God. This is what apostle Paul was saying when he said in 1 Corinthians 2:16 "Who hath known the mind of the Lord, that he may instruct him? But we have the mind of Christ." Another version says, "who knows enough to teach him?" NLT.

The word "That he will instruct" here in the Bible is a Greek word "Sumbibazo" which means to put or unite, gather, conclude… It means you have been placed on a level where you help God put things together. You gather things for God, and help God conclude matters on the earth. This Greek word "Sumbibazo" has only one occurrence in the Bible, and the Hebrew parallel meaning is Genesis 1:1 "In the beginning, God created the heaven and the earth". Which means that what Apostle Paul was saying in 1 Corinthians 2:16 is that you get to create as God created in the beginning. That's exactly what it means, "That he will instruct" that he will create like God created in the beginning.

You are at the level of advising God on matters; in this highest level of knowing God, you are called into his Counsel of Elders, where matters are adjudicated, and you will be able to speak and contribute to the decision makings in the Kingdom. This is where God begins to consult you on matters, as he consulted Abraham when he planned to destroy Sodom and Gomorrah in Genesis 18:16-20.

In this level of knowing God, your spirit is plugged into the Spirit of God, so you can think like God, and act like God. You will take the shape and the pattern of God on earth; an express image of God with a creative abilities of God will manifest through your existence. Your decisions will become Godly at every ramification, and no man can judge you because you represent God on earth. This is when you can rise and speak like Jesus did "Lo I come in the volume of the book, it is written of me to do thy will oh God" (Hebrew 10:7). You must walk according to your purpose on the earth to be able to get to this level spiritually.

If the seven lamps burning before the throne of God in heaven, represent the Seven Spirits of God, it means that the candle stick that is burning in you which represents your own spirit, must be plugged into the burning lamps at every level to get access to the Knowledge of God. In other words, knowing God at any level, entails being plugged into his own Spirit, which is the burning lamps before the throne. You can never achieve anything or progress into the kingdom of God without the Holy Spirit. The earlier you make him your friend, the better and easier the journey to your destiny becomes.

CHAPTER THREE

WHOSE IMAGE ARE YOU?

$\int$ ESUS IS THE EXPRESS IMAGE of God the Father as stated in the book of Hebrew 1:3.

An image is the representation of a person, either by a photograph or by a drawing. Images are drawings configured to represent a person or a thing. Many times, we hear that an image is made in the spiritual realm, and this image answer to the name of the person it represents.

Wrong images are very dangerous to make of someone, because when an express image is made of a person, that image becomes the perfect expression of that person.

In the book of Genesis 1:26, for the first time we could hear God in agreement with Himself, and His Government to make an Image of Himself on the earth. According to God, this Image will be called man and would represent him (God) on earth.

The word image here is a Hebrew word Tselem: which means a replica, a resemblance, a representative, an idol. And the word likeness in Genesis 1:26 is the word dmuwth (dem-ooth). Which means a model, shape, figure, form and pattern. In other words, man was not only created in the Image of God but was also created to take the shape and the pattern of God, to model like God on the earth.

David further educated us about the true meaning of Genesis 1:26, he said that God gave dominion to man over all the works of His hands, (Psalm 8:6). This means that man has dominion over everything God created on the earth.

Have you ever wondered about the true meaning of dominion? The word dominion there in Genesis 1:26 is the Hebrew word radah (Raw-daw). It's a root word that means to tread down, subjugate, prevail over. It then means that even God was aware of what was around the man he created, but he (God) charged man to make sure he prevails, subjugate and tread down, the works of his hands, including the old serpent. It was man that took lightly what he was placed in the garden to do.

It would interest you to know that when Adam began to procreate, the Bible said he begat sons in his own image, (Genesis 5:3), which was the corrupted image; this image was different from the original image he had in the garden. This means that once sin entered the man that God created, he (man) lost the image that God gave to him and took on another image. The sinful nature (Image). And Adam's procreation was then done in the latter image, the sinful image. As you read further, you will discover that why Jesus came was to redeem man back to the original image, the glorious expression of God.

Permit me to also tell you that it was for this very reason that God entered the Garden in Genesis 3:8 to take a walk like he always did in the cool of the day, to see a replica of himself. God would walk into the garden in fantasy in the cool of the day, just to admire his prototype, his own very image, his idol, the Man he created. Oh yes! man was God's own way of idolizing himself, it went wrong, that is why God has warned and continues to warn us his children not to make an idol or image of anything, he is a jealous God.

God would come in the cool of the day, to have a relationship and a communion with the man he created in his image. That evening, God entered the garden in anticipation, with excitement, having prepared a conversation he would have with man (and the evening and the morning was the first day), but the man he created in his image was not in the garden, God met a different image, the sinful image.

The evening represents the birthing time for the morning or the next day as the Bible would call it. You remember when God was creating, at the end of his daily creation, the bible would end it with the phrase, "And the evening and the morning was…" Genesis 1:5. It means that God began his creations in the evening which proceeded the following morning; God created the things he saw for the next day, the evening prior to that morning. When he said, "let there be light" in Genesis 1:3, that light was created in the evening proceeding the morning. And in the morning was when he verified his daily creation that the light appeared, and he sanctioned and confirmed what he saw with the words of his mouth. You know, the bible said that God saw the light it was good, he then divided the light from the darkness, called it day, and called the darkness night, Genesis 1:4-5. It was in the morning that he verified that when he commanded the day to be the light, that it was indeed the light.

To God, evening usually proceeds the morning, and it is in the evening that you create what you want to see the following morning. In other words, evenings are for creating, and mornings are for verifications of what was created.

Therefore, when God asked Job, "have thou commanded the morning since your days began?" He was questioning Job on the usage of his creative abilities. God was literally asking Job about his own creative abilities as a man made in God's own image. I hear God say to Job, what did you do with your own creative abilities as a man made in the image of God?

In other words, Job watched Satan use his destructive abilities against him, and God was watching to see what Job would do in response to the destructive works of Satan. Rather than respond properly like the book of Genesis 1:2-3, Job went with the flow; God called this kind of reasoning a "darkened counsel without knowledge" Job 38:2

Have you ever commanded the morning to the extent that the dawn would know it's place? (Job 38:12). What was God expecting from Job? He expected him to do what he (God) did in the book of Genesis 1:3. Listen well Child

11

of God, you must understand who Job was before this incidence. Job was a man who sat among the council of elders at the gate of the city where he lived. He was a man that elders would seat and listen to in awe and young men trembled at his level of wisdom. In other words, if God called him a perfect man (Job 1:8), it means he was indeed perfect. If God who is wisdom himself would call someone perfect, what do you think? Friends, read the book of Job chapter 29, then you will see who the man Job was before Satan destroyed his household.

Having a wrong image is the most dangerous thing that could ever happen to anyone, because people always and easily remember the bad things and not the good ones. The book of Job is a very good example of this statement. Child of God, once you mention the book of Job to anyone, what automatically comes to mind is sufferings and destructions. The image people have of the book of Job, has distorted their thoughts to the point that, many don't know who the man Job was or what he was after his sufferings, when God restored him. As I said earlier, when you read the book of Job 29, you will have a clear picture of who he was before he was attacked by the devil.

Then when you read further, Job chapter 42:12-17, you will understand that Job's life was better at the latter end than it was both in the beginning and in the middle. Wrong image is simply the darkening of one's understanding.

As I was saying, the evening to God is when creations happen, and the morning was when you verify your creation, your creative abilities, that's what God expects of us his own children.

On that very evening when God descended from heaven, his anticipation was to visit man that reminded him about himself, and the works of his hands, his level of intelligence, and creative abilities. The man that God created was his own fantasy; David who had a glimpse of the Fantasy of God over man asked God a question "what is man that thou are mindful of him, the son of man that thou visited him?" Psalm 8:4.

David after he understood this aspect of God's love and fantasy over man, he had to ask God that question. This love was also made manifest when he gave up his only begotten son to redeem man back to Himself.

Let me tell you the truth, if you understand what an image means, then you would do anything humanly possible to preserve your image. You don't want your image messed up, the sin at the Garden of Eden distorted the image of God which is man. Therefore, God had to give up his only begotten son Jesus, to redeem his image back to himself.

Have you ever taken a picture or a portrait of yourself that you admire so much, to hang on the wall, where you would easily see it? Maybe in your living room or your dining area or even your bedroom? Somewhere so close that you get to look at it very often? that's what you represent to God. You are an important portrait of his, an image that he admired so much, that he had to always come down to earth in the cool of the evening to admire his replica, and to have a conversation with himself, the man that represents him on earth, that is how much God loves man.

This was what God did, in other to preserve this very image, and incorruptible image that was corrupted, he had to give himself in the very express image of himself, the man called Jesus had to come.

As I said earlier, when God entered the garden, He said to Adam "where are you?" (Genesis 3:9), because he couldn't perceive Adam, he was hiding from God. All God could perceive was a corruptible image which was what lucifer had when he was cast out of heaven. God cannot behold iniquity; it is the very thing that took Lucifer out of his place. God was unable to perceive Adam, what he perceived was the presence of Lucifer which was iniquity, corruption and eternal damnation. The image that God clothed Adam with was gone, that's what sin does to man. It strips man of that glory, the image that God uses to recognize man as his replica, sin denies man access to the presence of God.

The image of God is the Glory of God, and if you understand this, you will understand who you are, and who you represent on the earth. Let me take you further to the book of Isaiah 6:3, where God opened my eyes to see what I am telling you now.

You remember that Isaiah said, "In the year King Uzziah died, he saw the LORD? Meaning that before his spiritual eyes could open to see the Lord, the king had to die. In other words, there are certain times that our eyes are opened unto God, to see him, to see his Glory, his Image. In this case, both Isaiah and the Seraphim had an encounter, their eyes were opened to the manifestation of the Glory of the LORD.

Isaiah's encounter was seeing God in his regalia, he called it his train which filled the temple, (Isaiah 6:1). To Isaiah, the LORD was seated upon a throne which was in a Temple, but to one of the Seraphim's, his eyes opened to see through the earth, the Glory of God. While Isaiah saw the LORD in his Glory upon a throne, the Seraphim saw the Glory of the LORD all over the earth, these were two different visions and encounters.

In Isaiah 6:2-3, one of the Seraphim who stood above the throne of God cried one to another saying "Holy, holy, holy is the LORD of Hosts: the WHOLE earth is full of his Glory". The seraphim had an encounter where he was able to see the earth through the lens of God, he was able to see the earth the way God sees the earth. While many may see the atrocities of man on the earth, God sees the earth differently. This was what happened to this special angel in Isaiah 6:3. He saw the whole earth full of the Glory of God.

The Spirit of God said to me, what was it that the Seraphim saw which he referred to as the glory? He said to me, the man made in the image of God, is the Glory of God. This word Glory as represented here in Isaiah 6:3 "Kabod" a Hebrew word that represents the magnitude and the great physical quantity of God all over the earth. It means God has multiplied himself in great quantity all over the earth. The image of God on man represents the Glory of God. When you want to see the Glory of God on the earth, look at his image on you, and your brethren. It is this glory that the devil cannot withstand, that's what drives him crazy. Remember, his own glory was striped from him? Ezekiel 28:18, his body was burnt into ashes. Therefore, he is so jealous of man who wears the true image of God, the glory of God.

To deepen your knowledge further on this, let me take you to Isaiah 59:19 it reads, "So shall they fear the name of the LORD from the west, and his GLORY from the rising of the sun. When the enemy shall come in as a flood, the Spirit of the LORD shall lift up a standard against him".

What do you think is the Glory of the LORD here? It is the same word "Kabod" as in Isaiah 6:3. It is man made in the image of God, and it is man (Glory) that the Holy Spirit will lift as the standard against the flood of fury and wickedness that the enemy will bring into the earth. The Spirit of God told me that man is that standard that the Holy Spirit will lift up against the whiles of wickedness. In other words, we are that standard the earth and creation has been waiting for to manifest, Romans 8:19.

Furthermore, Apostle Paul said in 1 Corinthians 15:40, there are different manifestation of the glory in every creature. He said that the sun has a different glory when compared to the moon, and the moon differs in its glory when compared to that of the stars. And he wraps it up by saying that, even when the stars are considered, the level of their glory differ from one another, (1 Corinthian 15:41).

In other words, the glory of man is also different from the glory of other creature; the glory of man is the same glory that God carries, for man was made in the image of God, and after his likeness. Man is the total expression of the glory of the LORD. Meaning, when the Seraphim was heard by Isaiah saying "...the whole earth is full of his Glory" in Isaiah 6:3, he was referring to the presence of the sons of God all over the earth.

Jesus took it further when he prayed a prayer in John 17:5 "And now, Father, glorify me in your presence with the glory I had with you before the world began". The word Glory here is the same Greek word "Doxa" that was used in above scripture in 1 Corinthians 15: 40: which primally means an opinion, the expression of one's opinion in form of a manifestation. The glory that Jesus was talking of here, is the same glory that man was created with in Genesis 1:26. This is what the glory of God represents on the earth. Because Jesus stepped out of his glory, took on the sinful nature, and became sin even though he knew no sin (2Corinth 5:21). Jesus was heard praying this prayer because that Image as God the son was more important to him than life. The image he had before the world began is the true image of the Father.

CHAPTER FOUR

FOCUSING ON THE TRUE IMAGE OF GOD

ELISHA, THE SERVANT OF ELIJAH was very dedicated to the service of his master Elijah, but beyond that service, he was focused on an image apart from that of his master. He knew the God of his master, and as he continued to watch the things, and the miracles that Elijah did, he desired more. It was because he was focused on a different image, that made him discern that it was time for his master to be taken away from him.

Have you ever asked yourself who gave him the information that his master would be taken from him? And how did he know not to leave his master's side? How did he know to ask for a double portion of his master's spirit?

You see, when you are focused on an image greater than that of your pastor, your master, and your man of God, you can have a double portion, which is the fullness of the Holy Spirit. There is no greater portion than the fullness of the Spirit of God, this is what you will be transformed into as you focus on that true image of Jesus Christ, the Messiah. Jesus told his disciples, those that believe in me, the work I do, you shall also do, greater work (Double) than this shall you also do because I go to My Father. (John 14:12).

What Jesus is saying here is, at the absence of your master, you will have his spirit upon your own spirit, which gives you an edge for greater work. Not only will you manifest who you are, you will also see yourself manifesting the spirit of your master. That is literally what Elisha was asking for from his master, to have access to the spirit of his master. Is your master greater than Jesus? If your answer is no, then you know that the most important person to focus on is Jesus, and not your man of God. Please show reverence and honor your man of God, follow your man of God as he follows Christ, but never aspire to be like your man of God, unless you believe he is greater than Jesus. What I am saying is, do not limit yourself to a man, Jesus is the perfect image you should transform into. When you focus on the image of your man of God, he becomes your little idol, which will only consume you because you are now in idolatry.

When Jesus said in Luke 6:39-40 "Can the blind lead the blind? The disciple is not above his master, but he that is perfect shall be like his master". This was exactly what he was saying, he was telling us not to focus on the image of any man, because as man, we have limitations (blind leading the blind), but if we as his disciples will focus on his Image as the Master, we can attain perfection thereby becoming like him the Master.

Apostle Paul said in 2 Corinthian 3:18 "we who are with unveiled faces can behold the GLORY of the Lord, we are transformed into that IMAGE from one degree of glory to another, which comes from the Lord, who is a Spirit".

Generally, veiled faces represent distorted faces and visions, which is usually caused by sin. The sinful nature distorts one's focus; how you can perceive God and his image, and how you can perceive yourself. Because, if you do not have a clear vision of who God is, you can never have a clear understanding of who you are; your ability to see God as God, will give you a clear representation of who you are, and why you are on the earth.

In other word, Paul is saying, we are now people with unveiled faces, people with clear visions of who God is, because that sinful image that separated us from seeing God perfectly well, has been removed from us by the blood of Jesus Christ, the veil is broken, we have access to God, through Jesus Christ.

It is then a very bad thing to continue to live a life of sin, with this kind of life, you can never have a clear vision of the image of God, or the clear image of who you are on the earth; what you cannot see, you cannot manifest or become.

It is not a coincidence that Elisha asked for double portion of Elijah's spirit. It was because Elisha was able to tap into that revelational knowledge of God, that made him know the time and the season that his master would be taken from him. Elisha understood there must be more to what his master Elijah had, and he referred to it as the double portion of Elijah's spirit.

Just as a side knowledge, Elisha had already encountered the Lord before meeting his master, Elijah. Do you think it was a coincidence that God told Elijah to find Elisha, and anoint him to be a prophet over Israel? How does God pick a random person to succeed a major prophet like Elijah, if he had no prior knowledge of who Elisha was, and if Elisha had no knowledge of who God is? In 1 kings 19:18. God told Elijah that he had seven thousand prophets who had not bowed their knees to Baal. God always have people whom he trains secretly to replace people on the earth. Man is very unstable, and God knows that, and he always has many alternatives waiting to be used in replacement of any man who becomes too important on the face of the earth. If you understand this as a man of God, it will save you from your pride.

Look at what Elijah's response was, "What you are asking is very hard" but if you can see me go" 2 Kings 2:10. Meaning, if you are focused enough, and not distracted, you can have what you ask for. In other words, joining words with that of apostle Paul, as we continue to focus on the glorious image of Jesus Christ, without distractions caused by sin, we are transformed into his Image by the Holy Spirit, from one degree of glory to another.

Moses said to God, "If I found favor in your sight, if you can see your image in me, let me see your glory, (Exodus 33:13). Moses was telling God here, let me see what you look like, so I can know what I look like. The word glory there is a Hebrew word for "Kabod" kaw-bode. This word as I said earlier, means the magnitude of God's glory, his great physical weight, and splendor.

Can you see what Moses was saying to God here? God said to Moses, I know you by name, meaning I can relate to who you are. You are that part of me that I like to have a conversation with. Moses, being shocked about this kind of love affair that God is introducing to him says to God, if you love me this much, I will take advantage of this love, let me see what you look like, your make up, your heavy weight, your splendor.

Moses had been with God for a long time, forty days here, and forty nights there, on and off, even though he couldn't see God face to face, but God looked at his face during their meetings, the way he smiled, laughed and spoke. If you look at the book of Exodus 33:11, it says that the LORD spoke to Moses' face to face as a man speaks unto his friend.

Now, let me ask you, how does a man speak to his friend face to face?

When you speak to your friend or hang out with your friend, how do you do it? If you are a genuine friend, I believe you would be relaxed, gentle and carefree when you speak to your friend. This scripture literally says that LORD of the Universe was hanging out with Moses as a man hangs out with his friend. This scripture also is secretly telling you that, when it was time for God to speak to Moses, he spoke to him as a Man, he stepped down from his throne, and entered Moses's arena and had a conversation with Moses as a man would with his friend.

The LORD knew every part of Moses, he watched him closely; Moses had a spot in the heart of God, just like Adam did. Remember, God would come into the Garden to have a conversation with Adam, it was a regular friendship relationship.

When Moses's brother Aaron and his sister Miriam tried to rebuke him, because he married an Ethiopian woman, a black woman, the LORD showed up to defend Moses. In his defense, the LORD came down and stood in front of the tabernacle, he clarified the difference between them as prophets and Moses, who is not just a prophet but a servant and a friend of God. According to the LORD, Moses is a servant that he speaks to mouth to mouth, Numbers 12:5-9.

One would wonder if this scripture was real? That the God we are seeking to reveal himself to us was seen standing at the entrance of the tabernacle during the times of Moses in his defense, not only that, but he also spoke in loud and audible voice that they could all hear him. It makes you wonder what has changed? Even now that Jesus is here, we should have a better relationship with GOD.

When Moses failed to do what God had told him to do in numbers 20, the LORD felt betrayed by Moses (Numbers 20:12). He said to Moses, you didn't respect me enough to show this people who I am to you. After everything we shared together, after our negotiations, you advised me a couple of times, and I listened to you Moses, I came down to fight for you when your family turned against you, but the only opportunity you had to make this people tremble before me, you blew it. Numbers 20:8-12.

You know the most hurtful part of the whole thing that made Moses not to enter the Promise land was not because the law as many have stated or argued could not take him into the promised land, it was because Moses who was a recipient of mercy and compassion of God, refused to give out mercy and compassion in return.

Mercy and compassion represent Grace, and Moses didn't give it out when the people needed it the most. The LORD wanted the people to see his holiness, his other side that Moses had seen, his merciful and compassionate side, at least it would influence the people to reverence the LORD more, but Moses out of anger despised the people, and the LORD felt betrayed.

I know you still have a concern with what I just said. To clear your concerns, do you remember when Moses asked the LORD, "Show me your glory" Exodus 33:18, the LORD responded by telling Moses that he will be gracious upon whom he will be gracious to, and he would show mercy to whom he would show mercy, what do you think the LORD was saying? It was the same thing that Elijah responded to Elisha when he asked for a double portion of his spirit. What Moses was asking was a hard thing that no one had ever requested of the LORD, but God decided to graciously reveal Himself to Moses, and allow His mercy to swallow up the inequities of the flesh of Moses to be able to see the backside of God.

The Backside of God contains mercy and compassion, that is why God said, no man can see my face and live, because his face is a place of Judgement, and he could not behold any sight of unrighteousness.

In other words, whenever you feel that God is not acting as quickly as you expect, His mercy and compassion is at a display. Whenever the LORD turns to face any situation, there must be judgement.

Since Moses could not give out compassion that he received from the LORD, but rather he struck the Rock, he forfeited the Promised land because only Mercy and Compassion could take him there. Be sure to know this, man has betrayed God for a while, that is why God asked Jeremiah in 17:9 "who can know the heart of man?" For from his youth his heart is desperately wicked and deceitful. Who can discern what man would do next? Because he is constantly thinking of wickedness.

Jesus experienced the face of God, which is where His wrath lies, at the Garden of Gethsemane. And he was able to see the cup of the LORD's fury, what he must do to redeem man back to God. In other words, for man to be able to see God face to face again after the sin of Adam at the Garden of Eden, Jesus would have to drink the cup of God's fury. God was face to face with Jesus at the garden of Gethsemane, showing Jesus what it would take for man to return to God face to face again.

The Effects of Your Focus

The image you focus on, does not only affect you but can also affect your offspring. Follow me to the book of Genesis 30:25-42, when Jacob was ready to move on from his father-in-law Laban, they made a deal that Laban would give Jacob every speckled and spotted animal from his livestock. Laban being who he was, in other to deceive Jacob, removed all the specked and spotted animal from the ones that Jacob had, and gave them to his sons, and put a separation between his sons and his son in-law Jacob.

Jacob devised a means, what an invention! When you have grace in your life, everything you touch becomes prosperous. He took a tool and made specks and spots on tree branches and positioned them where the animals would come to drink water and then mate. He positioned these branches in a way that as the animals would mate, their views would focus on the image they were seeing, the speckled and spotted tree branches.

After a while, the animals started producing speckled and spotted offspring. Jacob grew mightily in livestock and had servants and many donkeys. Not only did Jacob's livestock grew much, but they were also stronger too.

Because Jacob maneuvered it in a way that the strong female animals who were in heat period would focus on the speckled and spotted branches in the trough, and when the weak female animals would mate, Jacob made sure that the spotted or speckled tree branches were not in their view. The weak animals ended up producing offspring for his father-in-law Laban.

What I am trying to say here is this, there is a supernatural force linked to what you focus on. You certainly become the image you meditate and focus on, which also in turns affect your children.

Child of God, as you focus on the image of him that created you, and called you a god upon the earth, and if you can see that image, you are transformed into that image; the true image of God, the expression of his Glory, thereby becoming like Him, a god on the earth. Once you can see yourself as a god because you focused so much on His image and your image has transformed into His image, you can then realize your creative abilities, your dominion abilities, your fruitful and replenishing abilities.

What is the devil trying to bring to your focus? What image is he harassing you with? It is because he doesn't want you to discover your true Image, the Image of the Christ whom you were baptized into. Apostle Paul said it this way, "...we have been baptized into one body...and were made to drink of the same Spirit" (1 Corinth 12:13). The devil knows that the day you will perceive your real identity, he will be in a deep trouble.

For an heir if he is a child, is like a servant, even though he is the lord of all. (Galatians 4:1). What am I trying to say here? If you are a child in the things of the Kingdom, if you lack the ability to be transformed into the true image of Jesus Christ, you are still a child even though that you are entitled to every promise of God.

Do not allow the devil to cheat you on your inheritance, develop yourself and dig deeper into the depth of Christ by focusing on Him, seek a relationship with God, let yourself loose before the Father, and let Him turn your life around by his Spirit.

CHAPTER FIVE

CASTING OUT THE DEVIL WHO KNOWS YOU NOT

Mark 1:34

THE BIBLE SAID THAT JESUS was able to cast out many devils and forbade them from speaking because they knew him. And the Lord said to me, "You cannot cast out a devil who doesn't know you." The word Knew here …is a Greek word (Oida) oi-da, a knowledge that is completely full. An awareness that is so full without a doubt. the Bible is saying that the demons, have come into a full knowledge of who Jesus is, they believe and tremble also that he is the Son of God, this is without a doubt that he has authority over them.

What am I trying to say here? The devils Jesus had casted out, had experienced him while he was in the wilderness fasting and praying for forty days and forty nights, and they had come to a complete knowledge of who he was. Don't make mistakes, whenever you are in a place of prayer, the devils are aware, and they do experience or encounter the fire coming out of you.

Jesus told his disciples "…this kind goeth not out but by prayers and fasting", Mark 9:17-29. In a place of prayer, you give the devils encounters, and when you come out, they already know you, because there are angels who are there to enforce the answers to your prayer. In a place of prayer, you equip yourself and reinforce the authority you have over devils, and all you do is say a word, and they will obey. This is because, while in a place of prayer, you were being transfigured into the true image of Jesus Christ. As you prayed focusing on him, you were being metamorphosized, and when they sight you, they see Jesus the Messiah.

This is the reason why the devil said to seven sons of Scarva, Act 19:11-20, "Jesus I know, Paul I know, who are you?" Have you asked yourself what were they trying to say? The same word "knows" here is the word "Ginosko" a Greek word for personal knowledge that results from experience. A knowing that comes from experiencing the person. It is the same word "Yada" in Hebrew.

The demons were literally telling the sons of Sceva that they had already encountered Jesus and Paul and are also acquainted in encountering them regularly. "Who are you?" Meaning, the demons they were trying to cast out had not encountered nor experienced them in the place of prayer. In a place of prayer, many transformations go on with you, especially when you pray right, and since you are transformed in the place of prayer, when you step out, the devils see the image of Jesus Christ on you, and that's what they respond to.

In other words, you cannot use another man's authority that you have not made yours to cast out devils. The sons of Sceva tried to make the authority in the name of Jesus theirs, but they had not owned it. You cannot give what you don't have. The secret here is that Paul was given that Name of Jesus, he inherited it by salvation, and he made the name his own. Then he could use this name because he has owned that name by Grace.

You cannot establish your ownership of the name of Jesus Christ without an established prayer altar, which comes with a consistent relationship with God. Therefore, Jesus said loudly, this kind goes not out but by prayer and fasting. In the place of prayer, you encounter God, you experience your Father, and you get to know who you look like.

This was also what happened to Peter when he tried to walk on water like Jesus, Mark 6:45-51. Peter saw Jesus' walking on water, and he got excited as usual. Peter is known for excitement, he was quick to act, quick to speak, but it is in his weakness that his strength could be seen, he was also quick to believe God.

Peter, having heard the Lord, said to Jesus "if it is thee master, bid me to come" Mathew 14:28. And the Lord said to him "come"

Peter began to walk on water, but the devil who knew him not, because he had not encountered him in the place of prayer arose at Peter. The water spirit asked Peter one question, "this man walking on that other side, I know, who are you sir?" And immediately Peter heard that, he had no answer for the water spirit just like the sons of Sceva, and he began to sink.

It would interest you to know that the seven sons of Sceva were from a priestly home. the Bible said that their father Sceva was a Jewish high priest. (Acts 19:14). That your father is a high priest, or a pastor does not give you a guaranteed success, you must know and establish Jesus in your life on a personal level.

Let me tell you something very important here, do you know that before Jesus came up to them walking on water, he had gone somewhere to do something? Let me take you back to Mark 6:45-46; the Bible said after he had sent his disciples away to get to the other side, he went up to the mountain to pray. This was where Jesus handled that water demon. it was in this mountain that he subdued these devils of the seas before he stepped his feet on water.

Also, just to let you know, Jesus didn't plan to walk on water. If you read that scripture very well, you will see that after he had finished praying on the mountain, he came down and for a long time, he was waiting for another ship so he can meet up with his disciples.

Just to clear your doubts, follow the Bible to the book of Mark 4:35-37. When they sent the multitude away, Jesus told them, "Let us go to the other side". And the Bible said, while they were going to the other side in own ship, there were other little ships around too. (Mark 4:36).

In other words, there were always ships there because it is like a city ferry center. It is like taking the ferry from Staten Island New York to Manhattan New York. It was not uncommon to find other ships there on that day when Jesus and his disciples were to cross over.

Permit me to tell you that it was a very common thing for group of people to either use their own ships or hire a ship to cross them over. On this day, they had their own transportation system, their own ship. And Jesus was in the ship asleep, because he got exhausted from preaching or perhaps teaching from the morning until in the evening. When it was the evening, he told them it was time to get to the other side.

The storm arose trying to stop them from getting to the other side, because the same water spirits called legion was holding a whole city captive on the other side. Since Jesus had conquered this other territory, it was time to expand his territories, but the demons holding the city of Gadarene in bondage despised Jesus's presence in that city. These demons called "Legion" knew what could happen if Jesus was to be given a chance into that city. The mad man of Gadarene was the one in possession of these demons, he was the carrier, a vessel that housed these demons.

Just to let you know, in every city, there is a man or a woman who is a carrier of the demons possessing the city. The same way also in every city, there is a man or a woman that could be in possession or the carrier of the presence of God that could be salvaging the city.

These key people, weather be a man or woman carrier of the demons or the carrier of the presence of God always lives and will continue live at the gates of the city. In other words, if you enter a city, through its gate, the powers controlling the city must know of your presence. And if you will take any city for Jesus Christ, you must first take care of the one who is in possession of the demons controlling the city at the gate.

You may ask how did I know that the mad man of Gadarene was possessed by water spirits or demons? Let me take you to that location in the Bible, in Mark 5 1-21. After Jesus rebuked the wind and spoke to the storms in chapter 4 of Mark, they made it to the city. stepping out of the ship at the gate of the city, the mad man who was possessed by these water demons called Legions (Mob of rioters according to Message Bible), met him and worshipped Jesus. As a side word, anytime you see a mob of rioters harassing any city, the spirit behind it is this spirit called legion, mob spirit from the water, marine spirit, a lunatic spirit, they are the same spirit.

Also, when you go into a city where you see people walking around naked, or living destructive lives, it's the same lunatic, legion demons responsible for that lifestyle. Arrest the legion demons, and the city can be taken for Jesus Christ.

Back to the topic of discussion, the conversation between Jesus and the six thousand demons started. When Jesus tried to cast the demons out the first time, the demons raised up an argument with Jesus that it was not yet time for them to leave the city, in other words, they were legal occupants of that city because they came in by invitation.

Regardless, Jesus is the master of all spirits, he still ordered them out of the man. But notice what happened and why you should know that the same demons that arose against them in the sea, were the demons behind the storm in the middle of the sea when he said to them, let us cross over to the other side, those same demons came against them at the gate of the city. Jesus insisted that these demons must leave the man (because the man worshipped him, a form of surrender, giving his life to Jesus), the demons pleaded with Jesus in the name of God? Can you imagine what wisdom, and magnitude of deceit? That's why Jesus said be wise as serpent (Marine powers) and gentle as a dove. These unclean spirits, seducing spirits called legion negotiated with Jesus for mercy calling the name of God, and Jesus had mercy on them. But guess what? When Jesus told legion they could enter the herds of swine, they dragged all the swine into the sea, about two thousand swine got drawn in the sea by the lunatic demons. In other words, the swine became mad, and that's how they got drowned in the sea. This sea was also located at the gate of the city of Gadarene, so these demons didn't leave the city. They no longer possessed the man, but they were still at the gate of the city.

This is how I know the legion was comprised of six thousand demons, the Holy Spirit told me that animals are not like humans who have souls and have the ability to house thousands of other spirits. Only humans could house many spirits at the same time, animals could only house one demon at a time, meaning they lacked that capacity to house more than one spirit at a time. A dog can only manifest as a dog, a swine as a swine, a serpent as a serpent etc. but humans could manifest as these animals when they get influenced by the devil. After the devil entered the serpent (the devil deceived the serpent first and gained access into its body to be able to go after the woman at the garden).

You know, the devil or Satan is a spirit, and without a flesh, couldn't not and will not manifest. In other to really go after the woman at the garden, he needed a body, a flesh, and he found the serpent at the garden. Satan had a conversation with the serpent first, and was able to market himself to the serpent, who knows what he promised the serpent that made him give his flesh to the devil?

As I was saying, this is how you know that these demons were water demons, because they went back into the sea, their original habitat. The catch here is, the smartness of the old serpent, the devil; he drowned people's businesses and caused a stir in the city. They caused a commotion in the city, and the people came out of the city to the gate where these things were happening. When the people came and saw the madman, though they were happy for the man's deliverance, but it cost them their businesses. They would have preferred the man be left alone, rather than lose their businesses.

What did they do then? the Bible said they gathered and begged Jesus to leave their city. In other words, they would not allow him into the city, he entered the ship and went back, Mark 5:17-21.

Jesus had mercy on the demons called Legion, then he could not get into the city to preach the kingdom of God to that city. Therefore, you never negotiate with demons, don't have a conversation with a serpent, don't interview demons as some men of God would say, just cast them out; that's the mandate.

It is worthy of reference that the Lord would not force himself on the city. The people rejected Jesus, and he had to turn back into the ship. Have you ever wondered why God does not interrupt on matters concerning man? God created man and made him a god on the earth, He gave man the earth to manage. Being a God that respects his principles, he cannot interrupt in your life. The only way God can act in your life is when you totally surrender to him and invite him to help you. Just like the madman of Gadarene, who came and worshipped Jesus bowing to him in total submission, that was when Jesus asked the demons to leave. And many other miracles that Jesus did, the people or their families would bring them to Jesus or would invite Jesus over.

Have you ever asked yourself how this man became the mad man of Gadarene? You know there are people who live at the gate of cities, who believe they hold the key to the city, most of them practice occultism, and are diviners. This is how they keep the key to the city, by soothsaying and divination. And you know the Bible said that the LORD "frustrates the signs of the liars and makes diviners mad…" Isaiah 44:25.

By the Holy Spirit I was made to understand that this mad man of Gadarene was one of those soothsayers and diviners who continued consultations with strange spirits until the LORD mad him mad. In other words, this mad man of Gadarene invited those demons into the city and was a vessel through which they manipulated the city, until he met his match, maybe a man of God who cursed him and he became mad. Therefore, Jesus gave him that assignment, to go back and preach the gospel to the city, because if he could hold a whole city in captivity, he has that God given ability to reach the city too, (Mark 5:18-20).

Likewise, the people of that city, who I believe the demons influenced into sending the Messiah away from their city in lieu of their businesses, they preferred their businesses, their sources of income, their financial status compared to salvation.

Many times, people have made ignorant statements such as, why is God not doing something about some certain matters? The point is, if you do not invite him by total submission just like the madman of Gadarene, if you don't allow him access through worship, you may never hear anything from him. He created the earth and created a replica of himself and placed him on the earth for governance and accountability, he would not turn around and squeeze the earth out of man's hand, until there is a total failure from man to manage the earth.

Jesus also said in Revelation, "Behold! I stand at the door and knock…open the door, I will come in…" Revelation 3:20. You see here, the Lord Jesus said he stands at the door, and he is knocking, and if you are able to recognize and open the door, he would come in and feast with you. The point is that he will be at the door, he will signal to you that he is around, then if you are able to humble yourself enough to recognize his presence at the door, that you need him, and open the door, then will he come in. Apart from this, the Lord is a gentle savior, and would not barge in on anyone.

In the city of Gadarene, the people rallied round and decided they do not want him to proceed into the city, being at the gate of the city, he was refused an entrance into the city. Could you blame Jesus if there were people's salvations tied to that very act? He offered to come in, but they refused him entrance. He, the Lord who owns the earth, was refused an entrance into a city, and he didn't force himself through.

That is why what is going on the earth is delicately dangerous. People are constantly under a demonic influence to shut their doors or gates against the only one who can save them. People are quick to accept other gods, associate with other religions and paganism, but once you start talking about Jesus, it becomes a fight.

Let me get back to the topic of discussion, on that very day, after the encounter with the mad man of Gadarene, this time around, Jesus wanted to get to the other side with his disciples, but he wanted to pray up first. As I just told you what happened before this time, how he preached until he was so tired, and didn't do his regular thing, praying up before heading into a city.

When he sent the multitude away, he told his disciples to go ahead to the other side. He was thinking that by the time he was done praying in the evening, he should be able to get a different ship to meet up with them. Let me tell you, it was not the first time he had left his disciples alone or would send them into a city alone apart from him. There is usually a way that Jesus would use to have his personal space and do some recharging.

When he finished praying, and came down from the mountain, it was already the evening. You remember that the first time in Mark 4, he had taught the multitude until in the evening? He learned a lesson, he let the multitude go on time to make out time to pray.

Secondly, Mathew recorded he got a message that John the Baptist his cousin, and his forerunner was just beheaded by Herod. As you read further, you will discover what really happened to John the Baptist.

So as Mathew would have it, once the multitude had departed and his disciples entered their own ship to the other side, Jesus went up to the mountain to pray. He prayed until the evening, then when he came down to take another ship to meet up with his disciples, there were no ships. The same demon spirits tried to frustrate him again, they made sure no one was at the coast that evening.

Mathew said in chapter 14:23, he was at the coast alone from that evening until about 3AM in the morning waiting to get a ship that would cross him over to the other side. When it was the fourth watch, which is 3AM in the morning, he decided to walk across to the other side.

When he got to the middle of the sea, he saw that his disciples who left almost twelve hours ago, were still in the middle of the sea. Not only were they being beaten by the water demons, but they were also exhausted.

As I mentioned earlier when I started this discussion, Peter being the easily excited one, asked Jesus to ask him to come, in other words, "make me a partaker of this grace Jesus". But Peter, didn't have the capacity to carry the instruction or maybe better said, that Peter lacked the capacity to house or sustain it.

Many people crave for the physical attributes of what a man or a woman has, without understanding that a capacity is built somewhere to sustain the physical things.

What sustains the physical is mostly spiritual, just like you see a beautiful building standing, no one usually sees the foundation of that building which is what sustains the beautiful building.

It is the capacity you build in your spirit that casts out devils, gives rise to healing and other miracles you see physically. This capacity is built in the place of prayer.

If you check out the life of Peter, he had almost zero capacity in the place of prayer. He had no experience in the place of prayer and would not and could not give the devils encounters. That is why when the water spirit spoke to him while he was walking towards Jesus, "The Man walking over there, we know, who are you sir?" And Peter began to sink. Devil is not a fool; he knows when you lack that locus standi. It is called "legal standing" your ability to appear before a place of justice, your ability to state your case.

You see, at the beginning, I told you that Jesus forbade the devils not to speak because they knew him, Mark 1:34. You would also see throughout the life of Jesus, most of the time he would silence the devils and just cast them out. They obeyed him, because they knew him.

And I have come to realize that in the time of Jesus, the devils knew and obeyed him more than the people, the Pharisees and the Scribes, even his own people.

Let me conclude by saying that, the capacity you build in the place of prayer, is what sustains your physical manifestation of the Kingdom of God. It is in the place of prayer that Jesus saw, heard, and was taught the things he used to do exploits.

Develop a prayer life that can help you build capacity to carry cities, then nations and then you can reach the world for Jesus Christ.

CHAPTER SIX

ANOTHER MAN'S GOD: THE GOD OF MY SPIRITUAL FATHER

THE GOD YOU KNOW, IS he another man's God? It was ok back in those days to call onto the God of Abraham, Isaac, Jacob, David etc. you must also remember these men were men of covenants and encounters, and for their God to work for you, you must also make him your God. Meaning, the God of Abraham, Isaac, Jacob, David or your father in the Lord must also become your God under the new covenant, otherwise you are living under the law. The covenant that is now valid is the covenant we enter based on the Blood of the sprinkling, the Blood that speaks better things than the blood of Abel, (Hebrew 12:24).

Let me explain this correctly, if you must work out your salvation based on the covenant that Abraham, Isaac and Jacob had, you must remember that these covenants were based on the establishment on animals sacrifices on an altar, which had to be renewed regularly or yearly. This is what the Jewish people still observe. In other words, if you must continue to hold onto the covenant that Abraham had with God, you must continue to obey the rules of those covenants. Apostle Paul said it differently, he said that Jesus did not enter a covenant by the blood of goats and calves (That's how covenants were established in the old testaments, Genesis 15:9-19) but by his own blood once and for all (Hebrew 9:12). This is how redemption was bought for all of us, and anyone can enter in based on the covenant of the blood of

Jesus. This is why Jesus commanded us to eat his flesh and drink his blood (Communion) and as often (regularly) as we do it, we are bringing into action his death and resurrection, or better said, we activate the covenant in the death and resurrection of Jesus Christ by eating his flesh and drinking his blood.

It's a very dangerous thing to serve another man's God without making him your own God. Aaron served the God of Moses, and never knew God on a personal basis. Knowing God here entails an experience, an encounter. Aaron just followed his brother accordingly, and never bothered to know that God who reached out to him as a priest. It is possible that Aaron would have known the LORD personally, he didn't present himself nor desire that opportunity to know God.

Joshua was different, he desired to know the God of Moses on a personal level, he would follow Moses to the corner of the Tabernacle and wait on him while he had a conversation with God. Joshua would wait at the foot of the mountain while Moses was gone to meet the LORD. Out of this persistent hunger to know the LORD, he was noticed by God.

How do I know that Aaron didn't know the God of Moses, he was rendering services to the same God, but didn't know him? Look at Exodus 32:1-5, when the people approached him to make them a god, he advised them of what to do, he gave them his professional opinion as a priest, and assisted them to form a golden calf. Anyone who had experienced the LORD would never think of doing a thing like that. When Moses confronted him, look at his answer in Exodus 32:21-24. He exonerated himself, his excuse was that the people requested for a god.

It is a very dangerous thing to serve the God of your father, and not bother to know or experience that God. This is because, once that man dies, or disappears, you will fall by the wayside just by any little storm, this was the situation Aaron found himself.

When God told Elijah to prepare to come home, Elisha also knew about it. It wasn't because Elijah told him, but because God also told him to prepare himself too. Elisha was intelligent enough to make the God of his master his God. This same God told Elisha, prepare yourself because your master Elijah will be taken from you.

If you go to 1 Kings 19:3 when Elijah was running away from Jezebel, running for his life, when he got to Beer-She-ba, which was in Judah, the Bible said he left his servant there. This servant he left there was very slow, and wasn't fast enough for him, he lacked the spirit of his master the prophet.

Backtrack to 1 Kings 18:43-44, after Elijah had killed the prophets of Baal, he told Ahab the king to go and eat and get ready because the LORD was about to send an abundance of rain. The servant whose name was not mentioned was asked to go and look towards the sea, he was not told by his master what to look out for, I believe it was by purpose. His master Elijah was testing his spirituality, his level of sensitivity in the spirit. But since he was slow, he quickly returned to his master and he said, "There is nothing". What could he have done even if he saw nothing? Look deeper or perhaps believe in the God of his master to manifest to him. But he didn't know the God of his master, and therefore couldn't believe in him. Elijah told him to go seven times, and after the seventh time, he got the message. By the time he did the seventh round of walking back and forth, the man of God had the time to pray for the rain. You know, if Elijah hadn't told him to go seven times, he could have been back and forth to report to Elijah that he couldn't see anything, and it probably would have affected the faith of the prophet. That's why Elijah told him to continue going seven times.

After this incident and am sure there were many other incidents that made Elijah conclude that this servant was slow. What am I trying to say? When God spoke to Elisha that his master Elijah was going to be taken from him, He also advised him never to leave his master until he sees him go. How do you know this you may ask? There were other sons of the prophets who were told by their masters that Elijah was going to be taken from Elisha, they came to notify him about what they heard, and what was his response? He said to them 2 kings 2:3 "Yes! I know, hold your peace." In other words, he was telling them he already has that information, and they should mind their business. If he already knew about God's plan, did you ask yourself, how did he know?

Elisha made the God of his master, his God, and knew he wanted an inheritance from Elijah. He heeded to the advice he received from God, not to let his master out of his sight for a moment, even though his master Elijah insisted. Elijah tried couple times to dump Elisha on his way, but Elisha said "As the Lord lives and as your soul lives, I will not let you alone" 2 Kings 2:2-7.

You notice what happened here? Elijah said to him to stay in Gilgal that the Lord sent him on a journey to Bethel, but Elisha would not. Then he told him to stay in Bethel when they got there, and he wouldn't. You know, Elisha could have said, since Bethel was a place of worship, he could just build his own ministry there and moved on, but he didn't. When they got to Jericho, he told him to stay in Jericho that God sent him over to Jordan, but Elisha would not either.

Finally, Elijah parted the river in Jordan, and he then said to his servant Elisha, you know you are a smart kid, what would you want me to do for you since I will be going away from you? You notice Elijah didn't tell him initially, that he was going to be taken away from him? Elijah had that in him, he likes to try people out before he hands something over to them. He did that to the widow of Zarephath, before he handed her miracle to her, he requested she should make cake for him first (1 Kings 17:10-15).

Pay attention to what Elisha requested, a double portion of his spirit 2 kings 2:9. Not a double portion of his power or his mantle or his demonstrations. Elisha requested for double portion of his spirit. He wanted a double portion of his spirit because he understood that his abilities to do the things that his master Elijah did can only be sustained by the spirit, not the mantle. He understood that if you acquire a mantle and you don't have the man's spirit, you cannot sustain the mantle by your own power. Elisha understood that the spirit in his master was the Spirit of God in measure, he asked for a double portion of that spirit.

You can never inherit a mantle of a man of God whose God you never experienced by knowledge. Elijah told him that what he was asking was hard, why? Because Elijah didn't have a double spirit. But the only way that this could have happened is to see him separate from him, and if he could see the body depart, then the spirit could remain with him.

Elisha already had a portion of Elijah's spirit, what he was asking was for Elijah to remain with him spiritually. But Elijah said, if you are focused enough to see when my body is taken from you, then you can have my spirit. 2 kings 2:10. In other words, if you're focused enough that your eyes could see it, then you can become it.

While they were talking, a chariot of fire and horses of fire came and separated them, but whirlwind took Elijah to heaven. The Bible said in 2 Kings 2:12 that Elisha saw it, and said, "My father, my father, the chariot of Israel and the horsemen thereof" and he saw him no more.

You know, the whirlwind took Elijah, so what happened to the chariot of fire and the horses of fire? Did they stay with Elisha? I believe they did. If you search further, you will notice later in his ministry, Elisha was surrounded by the army that came to arrest him, he prayed for God to open the eyes of his servant to see that they that be for them is greater than they that be against them, 2 Kings 6:15-18.

Elijah was taken up, but the chariot of fire and the horses of fire stayed with Elisha, and the mantle that dropped from off his master. When you get the spirit, the mantle will follow you. Elisha was not looking for the mantle, he wanted the Spirit behind the man, because only that spirit could sustain the mantle. How did I know that Elisha was not looking for the mantle, and that he wanted the spirit? Let's read further.

When he got to Jordan, he stood by the bank of the river, who knows how long he stood there? I bet he was confused for a minute. Then he remembered, the mantle was with him, but the most important thing was that the spirit of his master was also with him. He took the mantle and said, "Where is the Lord God of Elijah?" And as he smote the river, it divided. 2 Kings 2:14. This was the last time he called unto the God of Elijah, because he was confused for a moment. The LORD God of Elijah parted the sea for him, and once it worked, he was convinced that the God of Elijah is his God. That was the last time Elisha ever used the mantle, because he wasn't after the mantle, he was after the spirit behind the mantle. Immediately he proved that he got the spirit behind Elijah, he abandoned the mantle, never used it again. He then started performing miracles saying "Thus says the Lord" 2 Kings 2:21.

You remember the sons of the prophets were in Jericho watching what was happening because it was something they wanted to observe. They were waiting to know who the spirit of Elijah would rest on. Their masters, other prophets in the land were also praying and waiting in anticipation to see if God would choose them too to carry the spirit and the mantle of Elijah. When they saw Jordan river part in two, and that Elisha went through it, they said "Behold the spirit of Elijah has rested upon Elisha "they came and bowed at his feet. 2 Kings 2:15. This is also how you know he was asking for the spirit of his master to rest upon him. These sons of the prophets confirmed it.

As opposed to what Elisha did with his spiritual sons, starting with Gehazi, who was the only servant of Elisha whose real name was mentioned. Though Elisha tried so hard to teach him about knowing his God, Gehazi was so poor, and his poverty distracted him a lot.

You remember Elisha prayed for God to open his servant's eyes, so he could see in the realm of the spirit those who were for them. 2 Kings 6:16-17. And if Elisha's servant was able to see in the supernatural, why couldn't he progress to get to know that God of the supernatural? He was a son of a prophet, what was wrong with him getting to become an anointed prophet to carry the mantle from Elisha?

Back in Old Testament, God related with man based on covenant he had with their fathers, but now He relates to us based on covenant in the blood of Jesus Christ. The covenant that makes God relates to us one on one, is the covenant He has with Jesus. His life that he gave on the cross of Calvary, gave us access to God the Father.

In the Old Testament, God did deal with man according to the covenant he had with their fathers and Lineage. Meaning, if God didn't have a covenant with your forefathers, He would hardly work with you. There are very few people that God worked with in the old covenant that were not related to their forefathers. Example was Gideon whose father worshiped Baal, he had to destroy his father's altar of Baal before God could move forward with him.

Meeting the God of my Spiritual Father

In 2018, I went to South Africa to experience the God of Alph Lukau, in the process of experiencing this God, I had an encounter. Let me tell you what happened. As I went to South Africa, after one of the meetings with Alph Lukau, I asked God when I got to the hotel room to show me who I am. I asked God that I was interested in discovering myself, I want to understand me, to know myself better.

Guess what the Lord said to me? He said in a loud audible voice, "why don't you ask to get to know me the Lord God?" I was taken in shock, because I thought at least that I knew God.

Apparently, I didn't know God. Even though I was a born again, tongue speaking and did church like others are doing. The Lord said to me, ask to know me.

Knowing God here denotes an experience. God saw how excited I was about Alph Lukau and what God did through him, and that I wanted to know me first. But, according to ABBA, the Father God, the God of All flesh, He wants me to know Him first, because the only way I could know myself so well is to know who my Father is, that God that Alph Lukau knows, who has become his God, can also be my God if I get to know Him.

As a result of this conversation with God, many things have happened to me. I began to seek God just to get to Know Him. While I am getting to know God, I am focusing on who He is, His very Image in the expression of Jesus Christ. The book of Hebrew said that Jesus was an express Image of God the Father (Hebrew 1:3). While I focus on this Image of the person of Jesus, I see me in Him, I understand that I am a representation of Jesus here on the earth. I understand that, back in Genesis 1:26, I was made in His image and after his likeness, I was given a dominion over all the earth (Psalm 8:6), the works of God's hands. I understand that I am to earth what God or who God is to heaven, for as He is in heaven, so are we in this world (1 John 4:17).

As I continue to focus on the image of Jesus Christ, I am being transformed into that same Image from Glory to Glory (2Corinth 3:18). You notice I said from glory to glory? Because there are many shades in God, once you get to know Him as a loving Father, He will take you to another shade of him as a Just God. Once you have known him as a Just God, he reintroduces you to another shade of him, a merciful God, and so on.

Having said this, I bring you to this juncture just to tell you this, you can never completely know God. Maybe it is more accurate to say, you can never know God enough. He is too Big and wide, and to conclude one day as a man that you have known God, is an injustice to your knowledge.

You can say, you are getting to know God, rather than say that you have known God. Knowing God is experiential, and when this begins to happen to you, life will become different for you.

Whenever you are ready to start your journey of getting to know God, you will begin to have encounters with Him and of Him. He will lead you by His Spirit, and will begin at your level, not another man's level.

Daniel said that "they that do know their God shall be strong and do exploit" (Daniel 11:32). Permit me to say that you couldn't do any exploit, if you don't know God. The Hebrew word here for knowing God is the word (YADA), a knowledge that comes by an experience. When you have experienced someone to the level of being familiar to the things they can do or the way they act or behave, you can get to do an exploit with them. You can exploit God, if you get to know Him to a level. This is when your faith becomes unwavering, because you get to understand it's not about you or your own agendas, but all about Him. You don't get to prove anything to anyone because you Know that God can prove Himself.

Moses tapped into this knowledge about God, and he began to do exploits for God and with God. He was able to advise God many times against abandoning his people, (Exodus 32:11, Numbers 14:13); and God repented from what he had originally planned for his people.

When you get to know the Lord, you can give God counsel, because He will seek your opinion on certain matters. God said in the book of Genesis, will he destroy Sodom and Gomorrah without first, consulting Abraham his friend. (Genesis 18:17-19).

Notice what God said here? He said in verse 18-19 that, "I know that Abraham will become great... and will surely instruct his children right."

God is saying that He knows Abraham well enough, He has experienced him well enough to trust him with generational blessings of the earth. This is to tell you that in the process of getting to know God, He is also getting to know your thoughts and your heart, to make sure He can trust you. The heart of man is very deceitful, in the process of you trying to know God, he begins to try your heart, to search your reins to make sure you cannot flip or disappoint him like others have.

In the book of Genesis 4:2, the Bible said that Adam knew Eve his wife and she conceived and bore him a son. The word knew here is the same Hebrew word "YADA" that was used in the book of Daniel 11:32. A knowledge that comes with an experience of that personality. A knowledge of a person that would make one encounter that person.

Still in reference to what Daniel said in Daniel 11:32, I would like you to see how Moses did an exploitative demand from God because of the little knowledge he had about God.

Permit me to say that when you begin to know God, which means you begin to experience Him, you can advise God. Meaning God is so wonderful and knows how to carry a relationship well to the point of making sure your opinion count in certain matters. God the creator of the heavens and the earth, the one who suspends the earth on water, will in his infinite wisdom consult you on certain matters as it relates to you, your community and the wellbeing of your nation or even nations around you.

You can see from examples how Moses advised God multiple times, the Bible said that God repented of the judgements he had planned against Israel. One major exploit that I believe Moses did with the LORD, was his ability to see the back part of Almighty God.

God confessed to Moses how much he loves him, and how special he is to him. Then Moses began to make his demands on God. Read Exodus 33:11-16 to see how Moses Interacted with God face to face, the demands he made. And in verse 17 of the same chapter, it baffled me how God responded to Moses, telling him He will do exactly what Moses had said and that he would also give him rest because of how much he loves him.

Moses then said, "if you truly love me the way you say it LORD, show me who you are". Let me tell you what was going on here, Moses is face to face talking with God, he couldn't see God, but God could see his beautiful face. He can see through Moses and his thoughts, but Moses could feel him so closely but could not see him, because no man could see the face of God and live. Moses then took advantage of God's love and mercy towards him, and he requested to see God.

Could you even imagine the situation that Moses found himself? he had been with this God many times and occasions. He could hear him mostly, from the burning bush to the mountain tops. Now, Moses gets a moment where God is telling him he is special and precious in his sight.

Moses says to God, if I am this precious, can I at least see what you look like. How did I know that was what he asked God? because the Bible said he asked to see the Glory of God? Remember I said the Glory of God represents the Image of God, in other words, when Moses asked to see the Glory of God, he was asking for the true image of God, his physical image, his Kabod, his weight.

If you read the response of God in verse 19-20 of Exodus 33, you will understand it by God's response. God said, He would show Moses his goodness, what He is made up of, his packaging, his substance. God went further to tell Moses, that he will be gracious unto whoever he would be gracious to. Meaning that Grace found Moses, God was just telling Moses that Grace has found him. The most amazing part of this encounter is that God told Moses that "I will show you what I look like, you will see all my goodness, what I look like, you will see my glorious self".

He went further to tell Moses how it would happen. He told him, he would stand by a rock, and when He is passing, He would place him by the Clift of the rock, He would announce to him when He is approaching so that Moses is not taken unawares. And He said to Moses "I will cover you with my hand while I am passing, and I will remove my hand from your face so you can see my back, what I look like, because you are not allowed to see my face. Exodus 33:21-23.

In Exodus 34:1-4 the LORD gave him further instructions regarding their meeting for that day; in verse 5, the Bible said that the LORD descended in the cloud and stood with Moses there; in verse 6, the Bible said that the LORD passed in front of Moses, so that Moses could see his back as promised. In verse 8, once Moses saw the back side of God, he bowed his head to the ground and worshiped him. Moses didn't write that part of seeing the back of God because it is an information that is sacred even up to date.

Have you asked yourself why was Satan contending with the Chief Angel Michael concerning the body of Moses? It was because of this same purpose, a man who saw what the back of God looked like. Satan wanted the eyes of Moses, if he could harvest the eyeballs of Moses, he would be able to extract some information from it, he would be able to have access to what God looked like. A very sacred information that even the angels don't have.

The love of God towards man makes Him (God) vulnerable. Man, please love God because He truly loves you. A God that fashioned you in his very own image, please love God!

CHAPTER SEVEN

A PLACE OF PRAYER

Have you encountered God; and has God encountered you?

THE PROBLEM IS THAT YOU have been looking to encounter God, but you have got to know that God can also encounter you. How can God encounter you? That may be your very question, in the place of prayer. There are people that God answers their prayers immediately. As soon as they propose in their heart to seek the face of God, he answers their prayers. It is called an encounter. God can experience you in the place of prayer. The problem with man is that we are seeking to encounter God, it's not really a bad thing but before you can encounter God, he would have encountered you.

What I am saying is, for God to give you an encounter, he would have experienced you first. This is what it means to seek the face of God, it is done in a place of prayer. Before you open your mouth to say something you would have thought about it in your heart, and while you were thinking about it in your heart that you are going to say something, God begins to perceive that very thought. Your heart is a mirror before God, and it is through this mirror that God sees you.

Once you begin to encounter God, it is a sign that God has experienced you in your place of prayer. Any man or woman that would have a changed life by God, must have given God an experience in a place of prayer. Jesus in his understanding of how this works, lived the life of prayer, and he constantly said, I say what I hear my father say; I do what I see my father do. All these are as a result of Jesus living a life of prayer.

Let me make this clear, many at times your heart is secretly crying onto God for help, for salvation, for mercy. While your heart is secretly crying out for God to have mercy upon you to save you, God is encountering you, he can hear what your heart is saying, that which your mouth has not spoken out. If you think that you just didn't do anything before you encountered God, you are making a very big mistake. No man ever encounters God without first of all crying out secretly for God.

What am I trying to say? If you stay in a place for a long time and you don't like the place where you are, you probably have not given God an encounter. There are certain people that once they start thinking about a matter, their heart begins to yell for the presence of God, their heart begins to cry unto God for mercy, for Salvation, for grace.

Elijah the Tishbite, was in a place of prayer after he just finished the display of God's power in the Mount where he slaughtered over 400 prophets of Baal. He told Ahab that there will be rain, after that, he went to a place of prayer. Why praying on his knees with his head in between his knees he was giving God an encounter, he was telling God to send rain as He had promised. God encountered Elijah in that place of prayer, and as a result the rain came down heavily. Prior to this, there was no rain for over three years in Israel. When Elijah was on his knees with his head in between his knees, he was pouring out his heart onto God, who had to answer, and as a result there was rain.

Daniel proposed in his heart to go into a fast, seeking to understand something from God, he made up his mind, he proposed in his heart, that he was going to give God an encounter. As soon as he opened his mouth to say something, God sent Angel Gabriel with a response to Daniel.

Daniel was a man, that was known even in a foreign country for prayer, he got into trouble for praying too much. He prayed so much that even the people around him became offended at his prayer life. Have you noticed that some people don't want to pray, but when you pray, they are offended? That was

Daniel's case. He prayed too much according to the people around him. But that didn't deter Daniel, he was a man who didn't stop praying until he got an answer.

Hence, Daniel said, they that do know their God will be strong and do exploit. Daniel understood what it means to know God. To Daniel, knowing God is equivalent to strength, and doing an exploit. It means that if you are not strong and if you're not doing exploit, you do not know your God.

God understood this about Daniel, that is why when Daniel opened his mouth to ask, or when he proposed in his heart to seek to know something from God, an answer was sent immediately. Because God understood one thing about Daniel, in the place of prayer he would not stop until he does an exploit until he is strong. Therefore, once Daniel purposed in his heart, God released his answers via Angel Gabriel.

You can also understand this about Daniel, in the place of prayer, Daniel did not stop until God asked a question, why is Daniel still knocking? It was brought to God's attention that Daniel had not received his request, and that's why he had continued to give God an encounter for another 20 days. God had to send Michael the Chief Angel to go finish up that battle, and to make sure Daniel received an encounter.

God knew Daniel would not stop if no answers were received. Now I am telling you child of God, has your Father encountered you enough in the place of prayer? Has God encountered you enough to release the strongest angels to take care of matters concerning you?

There are people who cannot go into prayer without an answer made available to them. These answers, usually come in form of encounters from God or his Angels. If God cannot come by himself, he will send his angels to bring you your request.

Jacob in the place of Prayer encountered God, his eyes suddenly opened while he was praying, and he realized that he was in an altar of his forefathers Abraham. When his eyes opened, he saw God and he began to wrestle with

God, he held onto the leg Of God, and he was saying I will never let you go unless you bless me (Genesis 32:22-30).

Though the Bible said a man wrestled with Jacob, but Jacob understood this man wasn't any kind of man, otherwise, why hold onto a man to bless you when your father Isaac had already blessed you? Jacob knew he needed more than the blessings of his father Isaac, that's why he sent his wives, children, servants and his wealth away, because he was prepared to give God an encounter that night. He wrestled with God until God gave him an answer. A change of name from a supplanter to a man who wrestled with God, who got God's attention.

That is what you get in the place of prayer, when you give God an encounter, you get his attention. When you give God an encounter, he turns his head towards you. When you catch God's attention, he will show you what you need to do, he would tell you what you need to hear that will change your situation and change your life forever. No man gives God an encounter, without getting an attention from God, is your heart cry strong enough that God can perceive you? Is your prayer strong enough (faith) to get God's attention?

God said in the book of 2 Chronical 7:14 "If my people who are called by my name, shall humble themselves, and pray, and seek my face… then will I hear from heaven, and I will forgive their sin, and will heal their land". These are the exact word of God, and he will do exactly what he said he will do. Jesus took it further in the New Testament when he said, "…Men ought to always pray and not faint" (Luke 18:1).

You know the bible said, without faith, it is impossible to please God, Hebrew 11:16. And if you must seek God, you must be diligent enough in your faith, believing that if you seek him, you will receive a reward from him. It is your belief in the place of seeking, that presents before God as an encounter. That is why, you would hear Jesus say, "your faith has made you whole" (Mark 5:34). In other words, you purposed in your heart enough, to grab what you are believing God for. This was the case of the woman with the issue of blood. The bible said she continued to say in her heart, "If I can touch the helm of his garment" that was her heart cry, that was her prayer, and she continued to say it and it came through for her, Mathew 9:21.

The Intensity of Your Encounters

When you look well in the bible, there are many who had encounters differently. The level of their encounters determined their results. The changes in their lives and the surroundings around them were determined by the intensity of the encounters.

You could also see Jesus again in the place of encounters in the book of Mathew chapter 17. The bible said that Jesus had been gone for six days, and as a result of him being away for six days, his disciples (the inner circle), had to go search for him. Because they knew where he would usually be, a place of prayer. They knew the few places where Jesus stages his encounters. What am I trying to say? You can truly set up a stage and plan your encounters. As I said before, when Daniel purposed in his heart to understand the things revealed to him, that very first day he purposed in his heart to go seeking God's face, he was setting up the stage for an encounter. He understood what he was doing, and he moved forward with it.

When Jacob sent his wives away, everyone and his assets, and was left alone, he was also setting up the stage for the encounter he got that night. Whenever you prepare yourself to pray or to worship in spirit and in truth, you are setting up or staging a place of encounter.

When Jesus was gone for six days, he was already in a place of encounters, the top of the mountain was his stage for encounters. Permit me to truly tell you this, the mount of transfiguration was nothing new to Jesus. It was only recorded because the disciples participated. What I am saying is, transfiguration was a usual occurrence for Jesus, it was a normal life for him. Do you know how I know this? Not only because the Holy Ghost told me, and not because I have seen that happened few times, but because Jesus said it in the Book of John 5:19-2. He said, he could do nothing on his own, what the Father does, the son also does. Meaning, his prayers were stages prepared by Jesus for encounters. These encounters included Father showing up and explaining to him (Jesus) what he should do next. These encounters were in forms of demonstrations by his father.

In other words, the mount Transfiguration was one of those stages and he was being addressed by Elijah and Moses. Peter, James and John the beloved were just favored to have walked into one of Jesus' encounters. They didn't walk into him when he spoke or was being spoken to by Father, they were just given what they received.

Let me explain more, the Bible said that "After six days, Jesus took his disciples ...and led them up to the high mountain APART by themselves" Mark 9:2. Let me explain to you what the Holy Spirit told me happened here. Jesus would routinely disappear from his disciples to the Mountain for prayers. It so happened that he was gone for six days, up in the mountain praying. When his disciples began to encounter challenges especially with the issue of not being able to cast out the devil on that lunatic boy, whose father brought to them for healing. His three inner circle disciples came to the foot of the mountain and began to call on him. Jesus came close and told them to come up to the mountain because he was not finished with the discussion he was having with Moses and Elijah. You remember the Bible said he led them up themselves APART. It means, they came up on their own, but he was guiding them up unto the mountain top. He was literally standing there and directing them on how to make it up to the mountain top.

When they got up to the mountain top, the stage was already saturated with the glory of God, and boom! They were caught up with what was going on. Peter, being the outspoken one, began to prophesy. The Bible said that Elijah and Moses were talking with Jesus but didn't tell us what they talked about. Why was Peter other disciples not able to hear what they were talking about? In other words, what was Elijah and Moses discussing with Jesus?

Jesus often said, he could do nothing on his own, he could only do what he sees his Father do. Meaning that Father demonstrates to Jesus what to do, and what to say. How does the showing, and the telling happen? In the place of prayer of cause, if you have ever prayed deep, often a time would come when the eyes of your spirit would open to things, scenarios and visions.

49

And you would understand what to do next. Pray until something happens, until you get God's attention.

"Thy Kingdom Come" an Expired Prayer?

You know our Lord's Prayer was a prayer that Jesus taught his disciples to pray based on their request. Jesus disciples came to him after they observed that John's disciples prayed a certain way. The disciples of Jesus Christ trying to be like other disciples asked Jesus to teach them how to pray as John taught his disciples.

The point is, you must not pray a certain way, or a certain number of time before you hear from God. For a long time, the Spirit of God has been teaching me on different levels of praying, you ought to always pray. Jesus in Luke 18:1 said, "men ought to pray always and cease not".

Jesus taught his disciples how to pray as they requested, and he told them to pray a certain way. This prayer was according to their need at that point in time. Now, at the time Jesus taught his disciples this prayer, they were still confused about the kingdom of God and the will of the father. Hence, "thy kingdom come" was what they needed at that time.

Today, the kingdom of God has already manifested and the will of God which was for the Lord Jesus to die for us and reconcile us back to the father has been accomplished. This is where I will make the point that the Spirit of God opened my understanding to, he asked me, why ask for the kingdom of God to come? He said to me, the Kingdom of God has already come and manifested. He said to me, pray that your heart may open to receive the kingdom of God.

The Spirit of God cannot tell you anything that He cannot prove to you. He then referred me to the book of Mark 1:14-15. When John the Baptist was arrested and put in prison, Jesus continued with the same message that John the Baptist was told to preach. "The time is fulfilled, and the kingdom of God is at hand...believe the gospel"

Here, Jesus was literally trying to enlighten the people to what time it is, the time for the gospel of the kingdom of God. This I know because towards the end of Jesus ministry, when the people got interested and they asked Jesus, when can we expect this kingdom, and where can we find this kingdom of God? Jesus answering them said "The Kingdom of God is not something that can be observed...it is neither here nor there, Behold the Kingdom of God is in your midst "Luke 17:20-21.

I must tell you what the Spirit of God told me, He said to me, Jesus is the Kingdom of God, He came and manifested, but people are still in the past asking God for his kingdom to come. Ask God to open your eyes, then open your heart to receive his kingdom.

Therefore, Jesus said in Mathew 6:33 "Seek ye first the kingdom of God, and His righteousness..." have you ever wondered why that scripture reads (and his righteousness)? If the kingdom of God is not a person, why then say his righteousness?

In other words, Jesus was saying to his crowd, seek me first and my righteousness. Jesus was trying to tell them that he is the kingdom of God, and once you find him, then further seek his righteousness, and you will have everything else added to you. May your eyes of understanding be enlightened as Paul prayed in Ephesians 1:18, so that you may understand the scripture better and pray better.

The kingdom of God has already come; when you pray the Lord's Prayer, think deep, do you need to repeat prayers like the Pharisees, or you need the Spirit of God to help you pray because you really don't know what to pray about? Romans 8:26.

How often should we pray?

Apostle Paul said in 1 Thessalonians 5:17 "Pray without ceasing." And I am saying to you, continue to pray until something happens, don't just wait until you are ready to go to sleep or wake up before you pray. Don't stop praying, even if it's five minutes here and there, keep praying. Speak to God until you hear him speak back to you. The Lord Jesus Christ is a speaking God, he has a voice, and he can speak. Don't limit the number of times you pray; the Jews pray three times a day, and the Muslims pray five times a day. Apostle Paul says to you child of God, pray without ceasing! That's your power source.

We wrestle not against flesh and blood... (Ephesians 6:12). The word "principality" is a Greek word for archas. Which means rulers, the chief whose job is to determine who rules. This was the level of resistance that angel Gabriel met when he came to deliver a message to Daniel. This level of demonic entity is the one who makes the decisions on who will rule, the time and the seasons. This level of demonic entity can manipulate leadership when the church of Jesus Christ is asleep. Watch and pray child of God, stand complete in Jesus Christ.

Learning How to Pray

Have you noticed that people have made prayer very complicated? What is prayer? It's a communication between you and God. Do you know that one of the reasons Jesus' disciples asked him to teach them how to pray was because they noticed his lifestyle, how he would get up while others were still sleeping, go somewhere to pray?

They also noticed that most times he would be in a place of prayer for hours and sometimes days, before returning to them. They wondered what he prayed about. But one striking thing they noticed about Jesus was that, whenever he returned from the place of prayer, miracles happened, demons cried out for help, sick made well, diseases were healed. One of those occurrences after he finished praying, he came down and there was no boat around to cross over to the other side, and Jesus walked on water. Prayer gives you a level of control and peace, but many do not know how to pray really.

What is then prayer? it's a communication between you and God. In the place of prayer, you are speaking to God and God is speaking back to you. In the place of prayer, God opens your eyes to your life, then he can help you tackle your challenges. In the place of prayer, you focus on the true Image of the person of Jesus Christ, and you get transformed into this image. Prayer is not just when you speak in tongues, prayer is also when you study the word, when you are deeply engrossed in communion and fellowship with the Holy Spirit.

The Holy Spirit told me something that intrigued me while writing this book, he said to me "Have you noticed that people who pray too much don't have faith?" I didn't understand this at first, then he said to me that most people who spend hours praying alone, lack faith, and he continued saying that the scripture said that "Faith comes by hearing, and hearing by the word of God" Romans 10:17.

Many who spend hours praying alone without opening their bible are very poor in faith, and that's why they pray too much. It is the hearing of God's word, the revelation of the word of God that makes your faith come alive. That is what makes the word become flesh, before it dwells in you. What the Holy Spirit is saying to us is this, you ought to always pray, and as Jesus demonstrated on the mount of transfiguration, a place of prayer is also a place where you can have a conversation with the holy saints, a place where the word can be thought and demonstrated.

Now, don't forget that Jesus said, when the Holy Spirit shall come, He will teach us all things, He will reveal all things to you, (John 14:26). Let Him guide you and ask him to teach you how to pray. He is a person, and when you open to him, ask him for help, and you will be amazed at what he will do.

Next time when you pray, just pour out your heart, your life to God, and don't forget to listen after you are done telling him your life. He will in return tell you what your life is, because you may have a wrong view of your life.

Don't forget true worship; it's a form of prayer that God can't resist. The devil is afraid when you pray effectively, because "…the effectual, fervent prayer of a righteous man avails much" (James 5:16)

CHAPTER EIGHT

PREACHING YOUR OWN GOSPEL

PROPHET ISAIAH STARTED OFF PROPHESYING and telling people what he believed were prophecies, and suddenly, his cousin who influenced him somehow died. King Uzziah was Isaiah's cousin, whose table he sat at to eat meals. Meaning, Isaiah the prophet was among those who were at the king's table. And being among those who were at his table, he prophesied what the king wanted to hear from him.

Part of the reason King Uzziah became so arrogant after he grew in might and power was because he had many prophets who sat around him. He came from a family of prophets, and it influenced him greatly. The Bible said he became so arrogant and proud to the point that he thought he could also become a priest to burn his own incense.

The point I am trying to make here is this, if the king had good guidance and prophets who feared the Lord and not him, they would have guided him appropriately. It is a dangerous thing to intimidate prophets, they will tell you exactly what you want to hear, they will prophesy out of their own spirit, or your own spirit, and not the Spirit of God.

In those days, the kings would array in their glory and sit on the throne and have the prophets stand before them to prophesy. And depending on how terrible the king is, he would either accept the prophecy or cast the prophet into prison if he didn't like his prophecy.

The four hundred prophets under king Ahab

To further deepen your understanding about this topic, let me take you to the book of 1 kings 22:1-28, where Ahab the king of Israel who had peace for a period of three years suddenly remembered that a piece of land Ramoth in Gilead belongs to them. Before this time, back in chapter 21 of the same book of 1 kings, the same king Ahab through the influence of his wife Jezebel took away the only piece of inheritance from a poor man called Naboth, because he wanted to use it for a garden.

Naboth was lied upon and stoned to death under the influence of Jezebel, the wife of king Ahab. After that, a judgement was pronounced by the LORD against the house of Ahab. Now fast forward to three years later, Ahab suddenly remembered that a piece of land which was under the habitation of the King of Assyria belonged to Israel. Then he decided since he was bored for three years without wars, to go to war against the Assyrians.

The purpose I went through the whole story was to enlighten your minds a bit further, to deepen your understanding of the meaning of a false prophet and what makes one a false prophet.

The king was visited by a friend, a neighboring king called Jehoshaphat, and upon playing with words and relaxing, they both agreed to go war to recover Ramoth in Gilead. But they needed to inquire of the LORD according to the customs of the land of Israel before they engage in a battle. The interesting thing here was that every prophet (four hundred of them) who ate at the table of the king (Ahab) said the same thing, "Go up; for the Lord shall deliver it into the hand of the king).

Prior to the king perceiving a thought of Ramoth in Gilead and how to recover it back for Israel, there were some spiritual occurrences and negotiations concerning his life. God needed to get rid of king Ahab, because his atrocities were too much and unbearable. While the negotiation was going on in heaven among spirits and God whom all spirits bow to, a spirit whose name was a lying spirit came up and presented himself before God, saying he would do the job of convincing Ahab to go to battle, how? by becoming a lying spirit in the mouth of his prophets.

However, all the 400 prophets paraded themselves and prophesied one after another the same thing: victory in the battle. Jehoshaphat wasn't restful on all these prophecies, his spirit was still troubled, and he then asked, is there no other prophet in the land who could say a different opinion?

Then Micaiah the son of Imla was remembered. But the king said, he hates him because he always had a different opinion. 1 Kings 22:8. It's very interesting to know that the king would hate a prophet because he spoke the heart of God to him. This prophet only spoke what God said, and not what the King wanted to hear. He was also hated among other prophets because he always had a different opinion.

Furthermore, a messenger was sent to fetch Micaiah the prophet. And it will also interest you to know that when the group of messengers got to him, they told the prophet that all the 400 prophets had already prophesied to the king, and they told the king good tidings. And they persuaded Micaiah to make sure his prophecy aligns with that of the 400 prophets. 1 kings 22:13.

But the prophet said to them that as the Lord lives, he would only say what he hears from the Lord. When they got to the king, upon request, he told the king what he wanted to hear. Not sure if he was intimidated by the group of other prophets who were probably sitting at meat at the king's table.

The funny thing is the king didn't believe him when he told him what he wanted to hear, the king was angry with him and reprimanded him. Then prophet Micaiah had to tell the king what he saw, 1 kings 22:19-23. He told the king that a lying spirit went out from the presence of the Lord to corrupt all the prophets, seating at the king's table.

This is very interesting, how a lying spirit could influence all the 400 prophets but still there was one in the land who was not corrupted because he refused to be influenced or corrupted by the meat at the king's table.

When the prophet Micaiah told them what the Lord revealed to him, another prophet known as a major prophet slapped him on the cheek. 1kings 22:24. His reason for slapping him was that he said that the Spirit of the Lord revealed the thing to him. This prophet called Zedekiah said, "from where did the Spirit of the Lord went from me to speak to thee?" Meaning, since when did you start prophesying that the Spirit of the Lord will bypass me to speak to you Micaiah? Very interestingly undermining what God can do with others. At the end, prophet Micaiah was put in prison, but what he said came to pass, King Ahab didn't make it back, he died at the battlefield.

Back to the topic of discussion, when you are under an influence of the king's meat, you cannot see clearly and you prophesy out of your own flesh or spirit, but not according to the Spirit of God. Having said that, was Isaiah then a false prophet before the death of king Uzziah?

Isaiah was a false prophet before the death of king Uzziah

What do you think is the meaning of a false prophet? A false prophet according to the Bible is a person who prophesy in the flesh, a prophet who is under a foreign spirit, the flesh profits nothing, John 6:63. A false prophet is also one who prophesy many things according to his own spirit, Ezekiel 13:3.

How can you prove that Isaiah was a false prophet? He said it by himself in the book of Isaiah chapter 6:5 "Then I said, woe unto me for I am a man of an unclean lips…in the midst of people of unclean lips" the word unclean lips here, is the Hebrew word "Tame" Taw-may, which means foul, unclean. The foul and unclean is a spirit, the same spirit the Jesus addressed when he cast out demons, the same spirits we are still casting out today from people

You remember, Jesus would say thou foul or unclean spirit? Mark 5:8. In Greek word it is called "Akathartos" which mean an "Unclean". It is the same spirit that Isaiah said his mouth was possessed by. He said it with his own mouth, he said he was a man of an unclean lips, but after King Uzziah died, his eyes were opened. He was given the ability to see the only true God. After this encounter, Isaiah's life changed, he was then endorsed by the living God to be a true prophet.

You see now, the Bible said that in the last days, many false prophets will arise in the earth, it literary means that many are going to prophesy out of their own spirits and may be influenced by the spirits governing their environment. In Isaiah's case, it was a foul spirit, an unclean spirit which was housed by his uncle, King Uzziah. That unclean spirit was the territorial spirit controlling Isaiah's environment.

First and foremost, the qualification to becoming a false prophet in the story about king Ahab, and his prophets, was to be among the prophets who ate at Ahab's table. In other words, if you were a prophet, and you were not among those who ate at the kings table, you were exonerated, you were not under this influence of a lying spirit.

What does this mean? Many prophets have been subjected to false prophecy by a spirit, and they do not have control of it because of the people they have associated with or the environment they found themselves. The spirit that left the presence of God as a lying spirit influenced or possessed the mouth of all the prophets that were associated to the king Ahab, thereby making all the four hundred prophets false prophets. You can become a false prophet by association either to a king or another false prophet.

Isaiah was under an influence of a foul spirit, an unclean spirit before he encountered the LORD. Not only was he a man whose mouth was possessed by an unclean spirit, he was also dwelling in an environment which was under the possession of an unclean spirit. Isaiah made some dangerous points here that many look over and have ignored. What Isaiah is also saying here is that your environment has a lot to do with your prophecy. Just as your environment can taint the dreams you have at night; your environment can also determine the way you prophesy, and the things you prophesy about.

God told Abram, get out of your country, from your kindred, and out of your father's house to a land I will show you, Genesis 12:1. Abram was of the Ur of the Chaldeans, a very dominated idolatry community where strange gods are worshipped. Before God could bless Abram, to make him a source of generational blessing, He had to take him out of a place, a community, and family infested by idols. It would have been very difficult for Abram to hear right and become a blessing in such an environment.

Do you know that Sarah his wife was barren as a result of deep idolatry in Abram's environment? And when he finally left, he took with him his father's house (Lot and his servants) who were also Idol worshippers. God did not communicate to Abram again until he was separated from his father's house, which lot represented. Genesis 13:7-14. Lot had to be separated from Abraham before the Lord visited him, and Sarah his wife was able to conceive. Do you know why? Because even the people that were associated with Lot, whom he brought with him were also Idol worshippers. And as a result of their idolatry, Lot was also influenced into Sodom and Gomorrah. Have you ever asked yourself what happened to Lot's servants that followed him into Sodom and Gomorrah when he was separated from Abraham? Selah!

Part of the damages you are suffering as a child of God is what you are holding onto, you are still holding onto old religions and idols of your fathers' house. How do you prophesy a very clean prophecy amid idol infested environment?

Let's consider another point that justified the claim that Isaiah was a false prophet until he encountered the LORD. When Isaiah cried "Woe unto me, for I am a man with an unclean lip, foul lips" God did not say otherwise, and the angels did not say otherwise, rather, one of the Seraphim's flew to him with a burning live coal and touched Isaiah lips to purge him of his sins and his iniquity, meaning a deliverance was conducted for Isaiah, to cast out the foul spirit from his lips.

And he said to him, you are now made clean, his moment of deliverance. He encountered the LORD, he got his deliverance from being a false prophet, then he was able to go as a servant for the LORD. Isaiah 6:7-8.

Jeremiah the prophet, when he encountered God, he was told, he had been ordained and anointed from the womb, and sanctified to be a prophet over nations. Look here, Jeremiah was under a different atmosphere, and it made it easier for God to use him. All God needed to do with Jeremiah was to put

His words in the mouth of Jeremiah, (Jeremiah 1:9). Jeremiah did not need to go through deliverance like Isaiah, he was already prepared and sanctified from the womb, (Jeremiah 1:4-5). This should tell you that Jeremiah was probably from idolatry free parental lineage.

In Ezekiel 13:3-7 The Lord addressed the prophets in Israel who the Lord called foolish prophets, because they were all false prophets. "These foolish prophets have followed their own spirit and have not seen anything", (Ezekiel 13:3). In other words, prophets can prophesy out of their own spirits and not out of the Spirit of God. When prophets see out of their own spirits, they lie and become diviners. That's what God called it, a lying divination.

Back to Isaiah the prophet, from all indication, you can see that the reason some prophets preach their own messages is because they derive their meat from the kings table, and therefore must say what the king wants to hear. This was exactly the situation that Isaiah the prophet found himself when his cousin, king Uzziah was ruling over Israel.

Isaiah didn't get to speak for the Lord until the king his cousin died. After the death of king Uzziah, he began to see vision and encountered the LORD in Isaiah 6:1-12, his life changed, his perception changed, and he became a genuine prophet. This happened because he was able to see his real self and the people who surrounded him. Once he had this encounter, he separated himself for the use and the service of the Lord.

Eli's House

The LORD said to Samuel the young prophet "Therefore I have sworn... that the iniquity of Eli's house cannot be atoned by sacrifice or offering forever "(1 Samuel 3:14).

If you read this scripture very well, you will understand that God Almighty swore concerning Eli's house, that neither sacrifice nor offering could atone the sins of his house for ever. It then means that even the blood of Jesus Christ couldn't atone for the sins of Eli's house.

What was his sin as a parent? He did not advise and discipline his own children, (1 Samuel 3:13). You would then ask yourself, the God who decreed such Judgement upon Eli, who was a generational priest and upon his generation, has he stopped being God? When people defile his temples and his people, does he look away? Is he not a Just God still? If he judged Eli's house for their atrocities, will he contain the atrocities that other men of God and their sons commit in the temple? Many men of God, molest God's children, and sleep with women in their offices, right inside the Church of God.

Some, who call themselves men of God or prophets and even priests like Eli, have allowed worst things to happen in the sanctuary of God. And they claim that they live under Grace. If God of all flesh will put into consideration what you do in his sanctuary, what you allow your spiritual sons and daughters do in the church of Jesus Christ, you ought to be weeping and hide yourself forever because you have endorsed abominable things.

Moses

God said to Moses to go to his people in Egypt, He had seen their afflictions and He (God) had come down to deliver them out of the land of Egypt to a Land flowing with milk and honey. (Exodus 3:7-8).

Now, I want you to pay a special attention to what God said, He said, "I have come to deliver them" God didn't refer to Moses as a deliverer, God is the only deliverer. Whenever a man starts to look at himself as a deliverer, he falls into a big problem with God.

In Exodus 3:10, God told Moses specifically what He wanted him to do, lead them. Having said that, we know that Moses wasn't a deliverer but a leader of the people of God. No matter how close you think you have known or become familiar with God, never mistake his place in people's lives for yours.

Exodus 3:17 is also a confirmation of what I have just told you. Moses was not a deliverer, but a leader. Moses himself needed a deliverance too. How do you become a deliverer when you are running away from the same problem?

Many men and servants of God are looking unto themselves as a deliverer, while they need deep deliverance. God can use you to lead his people through deliverance, it doesn't make you a deliverer.

Also, God demonstrated to Moses what he should do to convince the people that God did appear unto him. The rod that turned into a serpent, the hand that became leprous, and the third which he told him to take water from the river and put it on the dry land and it shall become blood.

What happened between God and Moses here in Exodus 4:1-17, was a negotiation. When you read through these verses, you will see Moses negotiating with God in the place of the burning Bush. His negotiations were his prayers, and God's demonstrations were the answers he got from God.

If you ever prayed and don't hear anything from God, then you didn't complete your prayer, or rather you didn't communicate effectively. In Exodus 4:10, Moses began to tell God about his limitations, he was autistic. Moses had anger outbursts at times, because he had speech impediment, he used his hands most time than speak.

Did Moses Preach a different message?

Moses did a great job and was referred as the meekest man that was on the earth in his own time (Numbers12:3). But, at some points Moses preached his own messages. When you study the book of Exodus properly, you would notice that there were few things that God instructed Moses to do, that he didn't really do exactly as he was told to. For the purpose of this book, we are going to look at the one message that Moses preached differently that costed him the promise land.

When you read the book of Numbers 20, you will find out that when the people entered a desert place on their way to the promise land, they encountered draught, a place of lack, and thirst. They were not only thirsty for water, but their livestock were also. And the bible recorded that the people quarreled Moses and his brother Aaron (Numbers 20:3). The people contended with him, resisted him to the point of almost beating him up. The word used there is the Hebrew word "Riyb" and pronounced as "reeb" which means a striving in form of contentious words that leads to bodily struggle and injury. The people were so angry because they wanted figs, pomegranates, but they were angrier because they thirst for water. (Numbers. 20:5)

In other words, they moved so close to Moses and Aaron his brother to the point of almost beating them up, but Moses and Aaron his brother had to escape this angry mob to the entrance of the Tabernacle and fell on their faces. They fell on their faces because they were humiliated by the people they were leading. (Numbers 20:6).

God shows up and instructed Moses and Aaron on what to do regarding the water challenge that the people were facing. God strictly instructed them on what to do, He said "Take the rod, gather the people, speak to the Rock before their eyes, so that the Rock shall give his water, and you shall bring the water to them..." (Numbers. 20:8). The very intriguing thing here is the Rock giving his water. The LORD addressed the Rock as a person, and one could imagine why this same Rock was always with them to give water? Don't forget, the place where they were was a desert, a very dry place, and the possibility of finding a rock is very skinny.

Moses usually would have anger outbursts because he was a stammerer, he was slow to speak. Rather than speaking to the Rock, he gathered the people as the LORD commanded, and he rebuked them, saying "Must we fetch you water out of this rock?" Number 20:10.

He struck the Rock twice, not even once, but two times. And water gushed out of the Rock abundantly. This single action caused him the promised land. Because according to the LORD, Moses disobeyed Him out of unbelief. Numbers 20:12.

What happened here was strictly abuse of power. To God, these people were His own, and Moses did not need to discipline them. God took it personal when Moses got furious at the people to the point that he forgot he was dealing with God, and not just the people.

Walking with God is a very delicate thing, and you must be very careful of the tendencies man has. Man has the tendencies to be independent or act independent of his maker, especially when he has attained a level of success. Most times, these tendencies cost him the very purpose for which he is born or called into service.

When you walk with God, you must learn how to be obedient to instructions God gives to you, regardless of what your opinions are. If you consider this statement, you will also remember that this portion of the scripture could relate to what happened to Saul the first king of Israelites.

Amalekites laid an ambush and attacked the Israelites when they crossed the red sea and were recovering from that long Journey. Though the Israelites fought back, God told Moses to record it and make sure every generation knows about it, (Exodus 17:8-14)

This was the reason why Saul was given the mission of wiping out the Amalekites. But he used his own judgment too and it costed him the throne. You can read further about this story in 1 Samuel 15.

It is a very dangerous thing to observe in this generation, that many have gone away and are preaching their own gospel and are neglecting the gospel of the Kingdom. According to God when he addressed Moses, he said Moses acted in unbelief, (Numbers 20:12). It then means that many who preach their own messages are doing so because faith is gone out of them, and they no longer believe in God, and in the gospel of our Lord Jesus Christ. Otherwise, what else would make you preach a different message, a different gospel.

John the Baptist

In the case of Elijah, God gave him an opportunity to work with his presence, to be there with him, but Elijah decided he was done. As powerful as prophet Elijah was, a prophet of fire, a man who physically judged the enemies of God, he couldn't finish his assignment in the Old Testament and in the New Testament. Elijah was threatened by a woman, Jezebel, and he quit his assignment.

In the New Testament, God gave him a second chance, to become the fore runner of the Messiah, Jesus Christ. He also didn't finish his assignment. Let's look deeply at what God's assigned Elijah in the person of John the Baptist to do in the New Testament.

Starting from when the Angel named Gabriel appeared to his father Zachariah, in Luke 1:12-17. The Angel told his father that his son John the Baptist would be great before God, he would have the Holy Ghost from the womb, and would also have the spirit of Elijah and walk in the same power as Elijah.

He was also going to help to convert many of the people of Israel back to God and help in establishing peace in families by turning the hearts of the fathers to their children and those who were disobedient to wisdom and prepare the people for the Lord, Luke 1:16-17.

The book of John 1:6-7 says that John came from heaven to bear a witness to the light, and through his witnesses ALL men may believe in God.

Let us consider the statement that John made when it was time to baptize Jesus. In Mathew 3:14 when Jesus got to Jordan where John was baptizing people with water, John tried to stop the master from being baptized saying "I have need to be baptized of thee". But Jesus told him to just allow it to be like that for now. What does this mean? It means that Jesus didn't deny it that he needed to baptize John, but he just told John that the time isn't right to receive the kind of baptism that John was hungry for.

You remember that in Mark 1:7-9, John was preaching to the people and baptizing them, he told them that he is baptizing with water, but there is one who is mightier than him, who would baptize them with the Holy Ghost. In other words, when John was asking Jesus for the need to be baptized, he was asking him for the baptism of the Holy Ghost, the baptism of fire.

John was a little too ambitious here, he was already filled with the Holy Ghost from the womb, and it was not yet time to get the baptism of fire. Jesus would have to die first, resurrect and then ascend, for this kind of baptism that John was asking for to happen. John was literally supposed to have worked with Jesus, complete his own journey as one of Jesus's disciples, then return to heaven with Jesus.

He was to wait for Jesus, after resurrection, get baptized with the Holy Ghost by Jesus, then ascend to heaven with Jesus. Just like in those days of Elijah. Remember that John had the spirit of Elijah who translated to heaven without seeing death, how come he was beheaded?

That wasn't God's plan for John, but it was the plan of Jezebel for him. He promised him that he would behead him the same way he beheaded the prophets of Baal in 1 kings 18. Elijah quit his ministry abruptly because of Jezebel, went to heaven, and when he returned in the form of John the Baptist, he had to contend with the same spirit of Jezebel in the person of Herodias, Mark 6:17-29

The reason Jesus said in Mathew 11:11, "Among those born of women, no one has risen to be greater than John the Baptist; yet he is the least in the kingdom" was because John was filled with the Holy Spirit from the womb, which has never happened to anyone born of a woman during his time. Yet he is least in the kingdom because, he still needed to experience salvation which was what he was asking Jesus for at Jordan.

Let me open your eyes a little further considering this matter. Jesus understood that John was already getting distracted and not preaching the gospel of the kingdom, and as a result he made the statement in made in Mathew 11:7.

When the people that John sent to Jesus left, Jesus started saying to the crowd about John the Baptist. It was a side talk though, but he was asking John those questions not the Multitudes. Jesus said, "What did you go into the wilderness to see, a reed shaken by wind?" this question was directed to John saying, what were you doing in the wilderness when you were supposed to be preaching the gospel and preparing the grounds for the Messiah?

Then the second question which was also directed to John the Baptist was "otherwise what did you go out to see, A man dressed in fine clothes? Look, those who wear fine clothing are found in King Palaces" What then did you go out to see? A prophet? Mathew 11:8-9

What Jesus was saying to John here was, what did you go out to see in the palace? What were you doing around the palace? Did you go to see people dressed in fine lining? Then Jesus said, of course people who wear luxury clothing or fine lining belong in the palace. And he continued to ask John what did you go out to see around the palace as a prophet?

These were his questions to John about his arrest. Jesus was literally responding to John's request to come and rescue him from the hands of King Herod, that's why he sent his disciples to ask Jesus if he was indeed the Messiah or should they look for another. But Jesus refused to go rescue asking him these questions. Meaning, Jesus was asking his cousin John the Baptist saying as a prophet that God sent on a journey, what were you doing in the wilderness when you were supposed to be preaching the gospel? And what were you doing around the palace? To admire king's luxury and his fine clothing? How did the king lay hands on you if not that you were around the palace? If you were busy with the gospel of the kingdom, how would you have ended up in the king's prison?

The Gospel that John was supposed to preach

Jesus said to them, go back and tell John what you hear and see, the blind receive sight, the lame walk, the lepers are cleansed, the deaf hear, the dead are raised, and the good news is preached to the poor" (Mathew 11:4). That's what the gospel of the kingdom is, and Jesus was telling John, that's exactly the gospel he was sent to preach.

You remember that I said earlier that, John the Baptist was supposed to prepare the ground for Jesus? He was supposed to have prepared the people and watered the ground well enough, so that the people would be anticipated and hungry for the WORD of God which is Jesus.

In Luke 3:5, every valley was supposed to be filled with people, and the mountains and the hills made plain to accommodate people who would be gathered to receive the kingdom of God.

As a result of everything that John was to do in Luke 3:5, the resultant effect should have been Luke 3:6. "All flesh shall see (Horan, a Greek word which means to perceive)" All flesh were to perceive, discern and experience the salvation of God which was the Kingdom of God. In other words, the reason why ALL flesh did not receive the message of the kingdom of God as preached by Jesus was because, John didn't finish what he was supposed to do in Luke 3:5.

John had an unusual anointing for evangelism, he had that Mimshack anointing for territorial coverings. Don't forget what the angel that visited his father Zachariah said in Luke 1:15-16, "...he shall be filled with the Holy Ghost from his mother's womb, and he shall turn many of the children of Israel to God" the word many here is also a Greek word for above, exceed. In other words, John was supposed to work above the territories, and prepare them in readiness for Jesus' appearance. John had the exact anointing that was given to Lucifer from the beginning, because of his assignment. An anointing that can turn territorial valleys into plain grounds, that's what he was anointed with. This anointing was given to him to prepare the ministry of Jesus Christ.

John was then offended at Jesus for not coming to rescue him from the prison he found himself, because to him, Jesus should have rescued him from the prison, to continue with his work. The most important thing here is that John preached a different gospel at a point. At the very point when Jesus was in the wilderness, John was to continue to announce the kingdom of God appearance, which was Jesus. By doing this, when Jesus finished from the wilderness, he was to reap the harvest of John's ripened souls.

John understood his purpose because he was initially speaking to the people as led by the spirit, he preached about repentance in Luke 3:3. If you look at Luke 3: 4-6, he was to make every crooked place straight, and the mountains leveled, fill the valley with people. Do you know why that needed to happen? Those mountains were to be leveled to prepare a place that could contain the multitudes that John was anointed to prepare for the kingdom of God.

Jesus was there in the wilderness being prepared by the Holy Ghost for the ministry of messiahship, because he believed John was doing his own part. Truly, when John the Baptist was preaching the right gospel (pointing people to Jesus), he had his own disciples abandoned him for Jesus. That's exactly what John was supposed to do, point people to the real messiah, the one through which they can be saved. I believe he got a little competitive with Jesus, especially when his disciples started leaving him for the "Lamb of God" as he rightly announced.

The bible said in John 1:35-37 "The next day again John was standing with two of his disciples, and he looked at Jesus as he walked by and said, "Behold, the Lamb of God!" The two disciples heard him say this, and they followed Jesus.

Not sure what would be going through John's mind, to have two of his disciples leave him to follow Jesus, but again, if he really understood his ministry well, he wouldn't have been offended. That's what led to him preaching a different gospel, Jesus was beginning to get all the attention.

In other words, at a certain time, John left off speaking about the Kingdom, and preparing the people who were already gathering to hear him speak about the kingdom of God. John started to abuse the people he was to prepare for the gospel.

The bible said that the multitudes gathered, to hear what John had to say, and to be Baptized by him, but he turned on them. Look at Luke 3:7, John said to the Multitudes who gathered to be baptized, "You generation of vipers, who hath warned you to flee from the wrath to come?'

The people got confused, because they thought what John preaching was for them to prepare to receive the messiah, so they came to be prepared by baptism. Out of their own confusion, they then raised a question to John, "What shall we do then"? Luke 3:10. The multitude said to John, you told us to gather, make the mountains and the hills plain, fill the valley, and we are here, and you are now calling us generation of vipers? John, what do you really want us to do then?

John started preaching his own message, which was part of what got him into trouble. Do you know what John said to them? Let's read together what he said to them in Luke 3:11-14.

¹¹John answered, "Anyone who has two shirts should share with the one who has none, and anyone who has food should do the same."

¹² Even tax collectors came to be baptized. "Teacher," they asked, "what should we do?"

¹³ "Don't collect any more than you are required to," he told them.

¹⁴ Then some soldiers asked him, "And what should we do?"

He replied, "Don't extort money and don't accuse people falsely—be content with your pay."

John began to preach the laws of Moses to them; they were already used to the laws of Moses which couldn't save them and have been expecting the messiah that was promised to them.

The bible said that John's preaching got them even more confused that they began to wonder if he was the messiah or not. Luke 3:15 "...the people were in expectation, and all men mused in their hearts of John, whether he was the Christ or not".

John became a legalistic preacher who preached about what the people were doing, but what they needed to hear was about the messiah. Some would argue that John did tell the people about the Messiah, but I am telling you by the inspiration of the Holy Ghost that John's primary message was not about the law, or charity work, he was to prepare the hearts of the multitudes who gathered to receive the message of Jesus Christ, by telling them more about him rather than discussing the law with them.

John ought to preach Jesus to the people, he was to soften their hearts already hardened by the law, to receive Grace which was the person of Jesus. He didn't preach to the people about Jesus Christ to the depth of his purpose on earth. He preached the law to them, and that's why Jesus had plenty of problems reaching the people when he got out of the wilderness.

As I said earlier, John's message ended his ministry, because he left off where he was supposed to be, a fore front of Jesus, he was supposed to work hand in hand with Jesus. In other words, he was supposed to be Jesus's disciple, and not raise disciples for himself and compete with Jesus.

Jesus was not supposed to start gathering people and raising disciples, that was John's original assignment, gather the people, prepare them for Jesus, but he didn't. John went on to become a marriage counsellor, he reproved the King of his relationship, he was harsh to the people even though they still feared and respected him. He got everyone confused about who he was, and who the messiah was, including the king Herod too.

If he truly preached the gospel as was assigned to him, why would people be so confused about his identity? If you look at the book of Mark 6:20, the bible said the king Herod feared him, even though he listened to him, and that's why when Herod then heard about Jesus, he thought John had resurrected.

Jesus did things differently, his style was different from John's style, he came for the people and was with a different approach. His approach got John confused, but it wasn't his confusion that killed him, it was his bitterness against Jesus. Let me explain a little further, John the Baptist expected Jesus to go after Herod, and demand that he be released, and Jesus didn't, and it got John bitter, and depressed while in the prison.

In other words, when he asked his disciples when they came to visit him in prison, what Jesus was doing about his arrest, and if he wasn't informed about his arrest, he was told that Jesus was busy with ministry. Don't forget that John's failure put too much burden on Jesus, so he struggled initially until he raised his disciples to help him.

When John was told by his disciples that Jesus was busy with ministry, he flared up, and in anger he sent them to Jesus, demanding that Jesus should confirm his identity. John was out of control here, but this is exactly what happens when one is working outside his purpose. Let's look at what John told Jesus through his disciples in Mathew 11:3

"Are you the one who is to come, or should we expect someone else? "He asked this question because like I said earlier, he had expected a different style of ministry from Jesus, and he also expected Jesus to rescue him from prison.

Why didn't Jesus' rescue John to start with? John was outside his mission, and Jesus didn't come to look after, or baby sit John like father did in the Old Testament. What does this mean?

You remember when Elijah was threatened by Jezebel, in 1 Kings 19? Elijah took off, and he quit his ministry. God pursued after him for a while, but he was unyielding, then finally God told him to go and anoint Elisha, and others so they could continue his ministry. (1 Kings 19:1-21).

Elijah quit on God, and was relentless about it in 1 Kings 19, and in the New Testament, John the Baptist who also had the same spirit of Elijah, got arrested and put in prison, and his expectation was for Jesus to pursue after him just like he did in the Old Testament.

Jesus told John's disciples to return to him, and to explain to John the things they have heard and seen, how the blind sees ... the gospel is preached to the poor. This is the most important thing for Jesus, preaching the gospel. In other words, tell John that what he was supposed to do was to preach the gospel to the poor, and not going after kings, people and their relationships.

But, most importantly, tell John that it would be better if he wasn't offended, because it would become a curse on him. Mathew 11:6. I just paraphrased it here. Jesus said "Blessed is he who is not offended by me" what does that mean? It means, if John would continue in his line of offense, he is therefore cursed, that's what led to his death.

John was not supposed to have tasted death, but he changed his course, and went another way. I know this by the Spirit, that John wasn't supposed to have tasted death, and there was no record that John was to die that way. The record of John by the angel Gabriel, was that he would walk before Jesus in the spirit and power of Elijah, (Luke1:17), and the spirit and power of

Elijah was the one who walked into heaven, Elijah didn't die a hash death, he walked into heaven by a whirlwind (2 Kings 2:11).

Just like today, many are changing their course by choosing to preach a different gospel and have also changed the course of their destinies and ending into different destinations.

Let's now look at the few problems that Jesus encountered out of John's failure, as it was written in the book of Luke 3:4-5, out of John's voice should come a gospel to prepare the way of the Lord, make the paths of Jesus straight. In other words, to make Jesus's work of Salvation a smooth one. Even though Jesus would have still died on the cross, but he wouldn't have needed to search out his own disciples and sending them out to help prepare the people to receive the kingdom.

What am I trying to say here? It was due to John's failure that Jesus restrained himself and went back to seek out his own disciples. Just to clarify your curiosity, let's look at what happened when Jesus came out of wilderness. You remember that the bible said that after the devil left him for a season, Jesus then entered Galilee, and he started preaching the gospel which John was supposed to preach. What was that gospel? Mark 1:14-15 "Jesus preaching the gospel of the Kingdom of God saying, "The time is fulfilled, and the kingdom of God is at hand, repent and receive the gospel". This was exactly the gospel that John was supposed to have preached, pointing to Jesus as the kingdom of God.

Although, initially, John started right because the bible said, "In those days …John the Baptist was preaching in the wilderness of Judea, and he was saying "Repent…for the Kingdom of God is at hand" (Mathew 3:1-2), but he went off course. Notice that Jesus started preaching this same gospel immediately John was put in prison? Mark 1:14. In other words, he was waiting for John to preach the gospel, and once he was put in prison, Jesus resumed John's assigned gospel. And in that process, he began to gather his own disciples, Mark 1:16-17.

You would notice that the first set of disciples he recruited, he told he would make them "fishers of men" Mark 1:17. Why did he say he would make them fishers of men? Because that's what John the Baptist was anointed from the womb to do, fish for men, gather people for Jesus, for them to receive the gospel of the Kingdom of God.

You would also recognize that when Jesus gathered his disciples, he sent them out to be his fore runner, the very thing that John was to be to Jesus. And when he had sent them out, guess the message he told them to preach? The same message that John was assigned to preach, which Jesus preached to some extent. Mathew 10:7, when Jesus sent his disciples out, he said to them "As you go, preach, saying, The Kingdom of heaven is at hand" and in Mathew 10:16, Jesus also told them to be wise, but also to be harmless. Meaning, be wise enough not to abuse the people you are to preach the kingdom to, he told them to preach with compassion.

One would ask, why didn't Jesus pick up John's disciples rather than looking for his own disciples? Because John had a different style and doctrine from Jesus. In other words, John was training his own disciples based on the Laws, but Jesus had a different doctrine, he needed his disciples to learn from him the gospel of the Kingdom of God. You also may want to remember that at a point that people were accusing Jesus of teaching his disciples wrong doctrine, they accused him that his disciples didn't fast like John's disciples and the Pharisees (Mathew 9:14). And one time his own disciples started requesting that he teach them to pray like John's disciples, Luke 11:1.

What I am trying to say here is, John had a different doctrine and gospel, and he didn't preach the gospel of the kingdom of God, which was what he was divinely assigned to preach.

In Luke 3:5, every valley was supposed to be filled with people, and the mountains and the hills made plain to accommodate people who would have gathered to receive the kingdom of God.

Jesus entered the synagogue. In Luke 4:18, he began by telling them his Spiritual identity. And he began to preach to them, but it didn't go well with them, because they were confused about who he was, his true spiritual identity was in question, some said "is this not Joseph's son? (Luke 4:22). The message that John preached initially to the first set of people, didn't get to them, even though this was Judea where the Holy Ghost had instructed John to start his preaching. (Luke 3:1-2).

The reason the Holy Ghost instructed John to start his preaching from Judaea was because the people of Judea were very tough deep Jewish Religious people, they practiced the law to the latter, and were very hypocritical. Jesus being a Nazarene would not be recognized in Judea as the Messiah.

Let me explain further, Jesus was born in Bethlehem in Judea, and raised in Nazareth, a little town in Galilee. To the orthodox Jews, Galilee was a contempt city, because the gentiles dwelled in part of the city. And they felt that the Jews who lived in any part of Galilee were contaminated by the Gentiles. These Jews who dwelled in the city of Galilee were not even allowed to read out the scriptures in the public places because they were considered contaminated. Since Jesus came from Nazareth, he was not really accepted or welcomed by the people of Judea. Hence the need for John the Baptist to have done a deep work in Judea to proclaim to them that Jesus is really the Messiah. It is for this same reason did Nathaniel say to Philip "Will anything good come out of Nazareth" (John 1:46). Because to them, Nazareth would not be able to produce a prophet because it is regarded as contaminated by Gentiles.

The people at the synagogue were offended at Jesus, and they went after him, they sought to kill him before his time because the ground was not well watered for them to receive the gospel. Remember that I said earlier that John the Baptist was not supposed to be beheaded, that wasn't God's plan for John. The original plan was for John to work with Jesus being his fore runner, and his disciple; Jesus would still be crucified, and after resurrection, return to heaven with John.

Just as a side statement, the demons were busy preaching the gospel, identifying Jesus Christ in the synagogues, they were busy announcing who Jesus was, Luke 4:34,40.

There are many who have been persecuted and killed due to lack of wisdom, as a result they aborted their purpose on the earth. Many others are also failing because their own John the Baptist are also preaching different gospels.

When Jesus was to return to Galilee, remember his first gospel in Galilee? He was almost killed untimely, he narrowly escaped death, Luke 4:28-30. After he spent some time in Judea, he needed to return to Galilee because he must also preach the kingdom of God in Galilee. And the bible said that he needed to go through Samaria, John 4:4. Samaria was a city which was at the middle of the border between Judea and Galilee. It was also known as contempt city because the inhabitants were idolaters according to the Orthodox Jews. Samaria was avoided by majority of the Jews, but Jesus said he needed to go through Samaria.

If the bible said he needed to go through Samaria, it means he could have gone through another route. Jesus needed to go through Samaria because he needed little revival that could prepare the heart of the people to receive his message. The woman at the well, became Jesus's John the Baptist of her time. The bible said that Many of the Samaritans believed on Jesus for the saying of the woman which she proclaimed to them that "He told me all that I ever did" John 4:39. Not only did they believe in Jesus because of the woman's sayings, when they heard Jesus speak, they believed more in Jesus and confessed that Jesus is indeed the Christ just by listening to his words and his teachings.

This woman at the well of Jacob, evangelized the whole city, and out of her own little evangelism, the people's hearts were prepared, and they received Jesus when they heard him speak. The woman at the well did the job of John the Baptist, and the whole city believed in Jesus Christ just by the saying of the woman.

That's exactly what John ought to have done for Jesus, proclaimed to the cities saying this is the Christ, come listen for yourselves. The final point worthy of highlighting here is in John 4:34, Jesus said to his disciples when they were urging him to eat, he said to them "My meat is to do the will of him that sent me and finish his work". In other words, the perfect purpose to fulfilling one's assignment on the earth is not by starting, it is to make sure that you finish it well.

Many have started on a good note like John the Baptist, and were distracted, falling by the wayside. To stay on course and finish your work, you need to focus on Jesus, depend on him, don't live an independent life in ministry, it will lead into destruction. John lived and functioned independent of Jesus, but he was supposed to live and co-exist with Jesus.

Jesus didn't just emphasize on doing the work of he that sent him, he also emphasized more on finishing that work, for what good is it to start something and not finish it well.

John's father was a priest in the temple of God during the time of Herod the King of Judea. John's mother was from the lineage of Aaron, Moses's brother. John the Baptist came from the priestly heritage; but as a prophet, he was in the spirit of Elijah.

As John the Baptist, when you are in prison, don't go questioning Jesus Christ for his abilities; find out where you missed it. Did you preach a different gospel? You are supposed to be a forerunner, why become a marriage counselor? And like Jesus said, say it to John the Baptist what you hear and see; the blind sees, the lame walk, the lepers are cleansed, the dead are raised...the gospel is preached, Luke 7:22.

Regardless of who you think you are, even if you baptized Jesus, the gospel must be preached! The Church is Jesus Christ's not yours. The Lord will not sit around waiting for you, he will raise other disciples! The Church is matching on, and the gate of hell shall not prevail against the church of Jesus Christ!

Are You His Disciple?

Jesus was teaching the multitudes as the bible would call it, and while he was talking to them about his father, many believed in him, (John 8:30). When Jesus sensed that many had believed in him, he introduced a very important aspect of his life on the earth, which is making disciples of men.

Discipleship was a very important aspect of Jesus ministry on earth, it is through discipleship that the gospel of Jesus Christ was preached abroad. Without the disciples of Jesus Christ, the gospel would have been limited only to the Jews, and in Jerusalem.

The problem is, many have fallen by the wayside, and have lost the true meaning of discipleship, many have become the disciples of their man of God and not the true disciple of our Lord Jesus Christ.

Whose disciple are you? If you are the disciple of your man of God, you will obey, and do the things and the words of your man of God, but if you are the disciple of Jesus Christ, even though you are with your man of God, you will obey and fulfil the mandate of Jesus Christ. You will choose to do the things Jesus did, and the things he commanded us to do according to the word of God, not the word of your man of God.

Jesus said to those Jews that believed in him in John 8:31 "If you continue in my word, then are ye my disciples; indeed, and you shall know the truth, and the truth shall make you free". Continuing in the word is paramount to becoming Jesus' disciple. Meaning, without a continuous focus in the word, you cannot become his disciple. His word is his life, his word is his makeup, his word is his image, and when you focus on his word, you are focusing on his image, and you will learn to do things the way he did, and speak the way he did, and eventually become like him.

Don't forget the second part of this scripture which many have quoted out of context "you shall know the truth, and the truth shall make you free" John 8:31. Knowing the truth is in connection to becoming the disciple of Jesus Christ, which is only for those who continue in his word. In other words, you must continue in his word first, become his disciple, know the truth, and then the truth you have come to know will make you free. Many are busy chasing after the shadows of freedom and deliverance, but do not know that the very thing they neglect is the source of their freedom and deliverance.

Many are busy chasing after the shadows of their man of God, after their likeness, and have become like their man of God with all the limitations and impediments of their man of God showing on them too. This is the result of being a replica of your man of God, and not a replica of Jesus Christ, or a true disciple of Jesus Christ.

Elisha took on Elijah's spirit, but was his own prophet, he didn't reproduce what his man of God (Elijah) produced, if not he would quit like Elijah when they came after his life too.

Please, don't get me wrong, I am not saying you should not admire your man of God, I do have a man of God and Prophets that I admire so much, but my focus when I am with them or around them, is the picture and the image of our Lord Jesus Christ. And it is the image of Jesus Christ that I see in them, that I focus on mostly. I look through my man of God, and I see Jesus in him, and the Jesus I see is what I focus on, and copy. Anything that does not look like Jesus, I discard.

What does that mean? It means, as I am on the earth, taking a journey in the kingdom of God, I have some great men and women who are generals in the kingdom, who I admire. I look at their lives, as they manifest as the true disciples of our Lord Jesus Christ, I learn from the things they do, but with the image of Jesus Christ in focus, as a mirror and I relate to them based on the word, learn from them based on the word, and follow them based on the word of God. Anything to the contrary is within my own judgment. In other words, I look at what I am seeing in line with the word of God, and if it doesn't line up with the gospel of our Lord Jesus Christ, I discard it.

Apostle Paul said, "Follow me as I follow Christ", (1 Corinthians 11:1). Don't follow any man of God blindly to a point of no return. There are many things that are done in churches today that are unworthy of the Christian faith, stay focused in the word, that is the first requirement to becoming the disciple of Jesus Christ.

Jesus said, "Go and make disciples of all nations", (Mathew 28:19). Making disciples of all nations here is not an authority to turn people of God into whatever you want them to become. You make them to become the disciples of Jesus Christ. It is out of pride and pomposity that many men of God are making disciples of themselves. When you understand that it all about Jesus Christ, you will not focus on yourself so much to the point of reproducing yourself in people. Disciple the nations for Jesus Christ, and not for yourself. So that when you die, many are not ruined. If you disciple them for Christ, if anything happens to you that you must go to heaven suddenly, the structures you built will still stand, because the foundation is Jesus Christ and not yourself.

The problem when you make disciples of yourself and suddenly you are taken from them, they will fall back to nothing except your image, and only the image of Jesus and his disciples heal the sick and cast out devils. If by any chance you were not a disciple of Jesus Christ, and you were a fake man of God, then your disciples are doomed. It means, you left them with nothing.

Do you think I am just speaking out of my mind, let me tell you what the Spirit of God told me about what I just said? He said to me, "What happened to the disciples of Jesus when he was arrested and put to death?" he then reminded me how Peter denied Jesus, then after his death, he took the other disciples back to fishing business. Of which after Jesus resurrected from the dead, had to search them out in the place of their fishing business. Would you not wonder with me how could Peter after he walked on water, denied Jesus and went back to business as usual after the death of his master, whom he promised to follow till the end?

Some of you men of God and prophets, teach your sons and daughters to walk on your grace which was the same thing that Peter did, he walked on water because the Grace of his master Jesus was available. Once the grace you have as a man of God disappears either because you relocated to heaven or somewhere else, what do you think would happen to the disciples you raised for yourself?

They will all go their separate ways like they did in the time of Jesus. Because you will not have the opportunity to resurrect from the dead like Jesus to gather them together and teach them to wait in the upper room for the Holy Ghost. What am I trying to say? Give the people of God good foundation, which is in Christ Jesus, raise them to focus on the Image of Jesus Christ, not your image. You are raising confused Christians, who have no way to go except wonder around at your death.

Have you asked yourself what happened to the disciples that some of the great men of God who suddenly departed the earth? Some of them who made disciples for Jesus Christ, and not for themselves have their legacies living on, but others who raised disciples for themselves have scattered sheep. The problem is from the foundation, you build people on a foundation called Christ Jesus, and not yourself. There is only one throne in heaven, and it belongs to Jesus, and not you as a man of God, therefore, make disciples for Jesus Christ, teach the people of God the gospel of the kingdom, and not just your own doctrine and gospel.

CHAPTER NINE

THE PROPHETIC!

The Sons of the Prophets

THE PROPHETIC IS THE MOST dangerous ministry one can be involved in. This is because not everyone agrees and believes in the prophetic. God uses prophets to bring information down to man, and this information can be in form of judgments or reconciliations. When God wants to Judge, He uses the prophets, also when God wants to reconcile with man, He uses the prophets too.

In the Prophetic, the LORD speaks the language that man can understand, though may not believe. During the time of Elijah, the Tishbite, God told him to go show himself to the King Ahab and He (God) will send rain. Remember prior to this, that Elijah had argued with the King, and he told him that there would be no rain nor dew for as long as he is gone. Elijah didn't specify the number of years initially, he just told him there would be no rain.

Now after three years of no rain, God said to the Prophet to go show himself. The king searched everywhere including the neighboring countries for Elijah the prophet, not to make peace with him, but to kill him. When God told Elijah to go show himself, he did. On his way he met the king's servant, who didn't believe him, because of the situations surrounding the whole thing.

Elijah's Unknown Servant

Elijah said to his servant, let me teach you how to discover signs and seasons, he said to him, "Go up now, look toward the sea. He went up and looked and said there is nothing"

Why did he say there is nothing? Is it really because there was nothing or that his eyes couldn't, see? Notice something here, Elijah said to him "Go again seven times"

This servant of Elijah without a name was being trained in the prophetic by his master Elijah, but to his master, he was a little dull. Because, to see with the eyes of the spirit, you need to be able to have tenacity, you need to be able to have bifocal vision. Bifocal in the sense that you must have two-part lenses with different focal lengths. What does this mean? Two parts focal lenses have the ability to focus to see a distant vision and a near vision.

Whenever you lack that ability to see a distant vision, you are said to be Myopic in your vision (nearsightedness). You can only see things closer to you, but those that are at a distance are blurry to your eyes.

This was the case here with Elijah's unknown servant. He had a bit of a spiritual myopia which limited his ability to function in the prophetic when his master needed him the most.

Just as a preamble, Elijah had just finished a great and the most hectic job of all seasons, he conducted an all-day crusade where he displayed the power of God against the prophets of Baal. As a result, over 400 prophets of Baal were slaughtered. You can imagine what's happening here, the prophet was already exhausted from a day long crusade, and there is need for God to complete what he started with Elijah on the crusade ground. Fire fell and consumed the sacrifices on the altar at Mount Carmel, now there is need for rain to fall.

Elijah testing out his servant's prophetic nature (those days servants to prophets were also known as the sons of prophets), he sent him out to see if he could see what he the master could see in the spiritual. Prophets are known well for their ability to see with and without the spiritual eyes. That's what bifocal means spiritually, your ability to see near (physical objects) and far, (spiritual objects).

You remember when another son of the prophet who later became a major prophet (Elisha) was being surrounded by horses and chariots, and his servant (also unknown) came to him in dismay and cried out that they were dead men because of what he could see physically (Myopia). the Bible said that the prophet Elisha prayed "Then Elisha prayed and said, "O Lord, please open his eyes that he may see." So, the Lord opened the eyes of the young man, and he saw, and behold, the mountain was full of horses and chariots of fire all around Elisha. (2 Kings 6:15-17).

The young man as the Bible rightfully called him was able to see into the supernatural, and what he saw was like what he saw in the physical, horses and chariots of fire surrounding Elisha. What he saw physically were horses and chariots surrounding Elisha. Sometimes what you see physically may limit what is in the spiritual realm.

That was the case of this servant of the prophet, Elijah. When his master the prophet told him to go to up and look towards the sea. This was to test his ability to see deeper. You remember that Elijah already told Ahab to go up and have some food (because they had a long day at the crusade ground on Mount Camel), and that he could hear the sound of abundance of rain. (1 Kings 18:41). At this time Elijah was the only one who could hear this sound, but he wanted to wait through it. Therefore, he sent his servant to go become his eyes, while he went back to the same Mount Carmel where he laid the sacrifice to the LORD, where fire fell from heaven and licked up the sacrifice.

When he went back to the same mount, he got on his knees, and he put his head between his knees to pray. What was his prayer? The same prayer he prayed initially that made fire fall "O Lord, God of Abraham, Isaac, and Israel, let it be known this day that you are God in Israel, and that I am your servant, and that I have done all these things at your word. Answer me, O Lord, answer me, that this people may know that you, O Lord, are God, and that you have turned their hearts back." (1 Kings 18: 36-37).

That was his prayer, he was still waiting for God to send rain while praying this prayer, and his servant wasn't in tune with his vision. How did I know that? It is right there in the scripture, "And he said to his servant, "Go up now, look toward the sea." And he went up and looked and said, "There is nothing." And he said, "Go again," seven times" (1 Kings 18:43).

The prophet told him to go again seven times, which is several completions, if he didn't see anything the seventh time, it would have been a very bad journey for the young man.

On the seventh time, the Bible said he finally saw a cloud rising out of the see like a man's hand. Finally, this young man was able to see in the supernatural. Have you ever asked yourself a question, how was he able to see a cloud rising out of the see with his physical eyes? To the normal person, when you need to see if it's going to rain, you would look up to the sky, which was what natural eyes would see.

In other words, there is a cloud that rises from the sea first (spiritual) then the cloud that is seen on the heavens or sky (physical). The later was seen afterwards as was written in the Bible "And in a little while the heavens grew black with clouds and wind, and there was a great rain" (1 Kings 18:45).

The point I am trying to make here, as the Spirit leads me is, there is a seeing that happens spiritually before the seeing that happens physically. Unfortunately, to many, the latter is what they are used to, but the former, which is the spiritual happens first and supersedes the physical. In other words, the spiritual supersedes and will always happen first before the physical, if you can't see the spiritual or supernatural before the physical, you are short changed.

Believe me as I say this, the reason that Elijah abandoned his servant after this experience was because he was a little short sighted. He was spiritually myopic, and his master the prophet had no patience to continue to train him. Elijah was a prophet of fire but was also a man without too much of patience. There are many instances to prove this.

The first instance was this one that I just told you about; in 1 kings 19:3 after he was threatened by Jezebel, he was afraid for his life, then he ran, and his servant followed him still, but when he got to Beersheba, the Bible said he left his servant there and continued with his journey. In other words, even when the Bible said that the hand of the LORD was upon Elijah that he ran more than Ahab and his chariots (1 Kings 18:46), this servant of his was also running either behind him or with him. He was faithful in following his master but wasn't spiritually in tune as his master would have desired. His master the prophet, left him, dumped him, or better said fired him, and went his own way.

The second instance would be seen in the book of 1kings 19:19-20, where Elijah was to call Elisha into ministry according to what God had spoken to him about. After he called him, Elisha pleaded with him to please give him just few days to go and tell his parents goodbye (in those days ministry was a sold-out life, you have no side job or activities except the work of God). After Elisha requested for few days to prepare him for ministry, Elijah told him to back off. "Elisha ran after Elijah and said, "Let me kiss my father and my mother, and then I will follow you." And he said to him, "Go back again, for what have I done to you?" He literally had no patient for Elisha's request, he told him, what is my business with you?

Also in 2 Kings 2:1-2 "When the Lord was about to take Elijah up to heaven by a whirlwind, Elijah and Elisha were traveling from Gilgal. Elijah said to Elisha, "Please stay here, for the Lord has sent me to Bethel." But Elisha replied, "As the Lord lives and as your soul lives, I will not leave you." So, they went down to Bethel.

In other words, Elijah wanted to dump his servant at this time, which was Elisha at Gilgal, but Elisha who was spiritually in tune, he had also developed in the prophetic, God had warned him specifically to make sure he didn't let Elijah out of his sight. That's why Elisha answered him that "As the Lord lives and as your soul lives, I will not leave you." (2 Kings 2:2). In other words, Elisha is saying that the only thing that could separate him from his master Elijah is death, in this case by whirlwind.

God had already spoken to Elisha during his quiet time and in his secret place that he will be taking his master prophet Elijah away from him and warned him to make sure that he receives the mantle from him. Elijah was ready to take his mantle back into heaven, he wasn't ready to part with it.

Elijah had no patience for recruiting and sustaining servants. This character is also a prophetic life, prophets are not known as patient individuals, the fire in the bones makes them susceptible to impatience.

Gehazi: a son of the prophet was he greedy or hungry?

You know when the Spirit of God asked me this question, I was baffled. The Spirit of God started to teach me something new, and as he was expanding it in the word, he gave me a deep teaching on the life of Gehazi the son and the servant of Elisha the prophet.

The problem is that some men of God have dedicated themselves to making sure that no man receive of their mantle. They would always justify this very act to the argument that the sons were not prepared and not ready to receive the mantle or their blessings.

One would argue that if some of these men were not eligible for their mantles, were they eligible to provide the services they rendered?

The life of Gehazi has been used as a reference to bad sons and servants in the church. I was also guilty of referring to Gehazi as being greedy and seeking for something to fill his belly.

But, today, when the Spirit of God asked me that question, I was literally taken aback. Was Gehazi really a bad servant or was he in need or hungry?

Let's go deeper to this very truth. First, let me take you to the books of 2 Kings 4:1-3.

A widow, who was a servant to Prophet Elisha approached the prophet in tears begging for help. Look at verse one very well; it says that the widow cried unto Elisha saying "My husband who served you is dead, and you know how he feared the Lord... now a creditor has come to take my two sons as slaves" NLT.

Looking at this scripture, you would agree with me that Elisha had other servants before Gehazi. and they were poor and in debt. What could you argue to justify the fact that this son of a prophet who feared the Lord and did serve Elisha faithfully died leaving his widow and two sons without any inheritance? Was that right? I leave you with the answer.

Many times, people especially men of God when they want to reprimand their sons in the faith refer them to the story of Gehazi and how his generation was cursed because of his action.

It would benefit you to know that at the time when this incident was happening to this widow, Gehazi was there with Elisha. How did you know that? Because Gehazi was Elisha's servant, and for anyone to see the prophet, you would have to go through his servant. In other words, Gehazi watched what happened to this widow with her two sons. Also, permit me to say to you that it was at the point where it was bad that Gehazi offered to allow the widow to see the prophet, Elisha. Because Gehazi restricted people from seeing the prophet, it was his job. If you look at 2 kings 4:27 when the Shunamite woman whose son was dead coming to prophet Elisha's feet, Gehazi quickly came near to thrust her away, but Elisha the prophet told him to leave her alone.

In other words, Gehazi knew the story of this woman and watching her go through this mess was frightening to him. Could you imagine a fellow servant whom you worked with, die and now his sons were being taken over by debtors? Did you think that perhaps, Gehazi also had some debts because he had a family and a wife to take care of?

Let me bring your thoughts to what the Holy Spirit told me; the sons of the prophets devoted all their lives serving the prophet if they had to be the sons or servants of the prophets.

How can you prove this? You remember when Elijah put his mantle on Elisha to call him to become his son? The Bible said he was plowing his father's field, meaning he had a job, and he had a sustainable source of income. When Elijah beckoned on him, he told him "Please give me some time to put my house in order, let me kiss my father and mother goodbye" 1 kings 19:19-21. Meaning that Elisha wasn't married, and he had no Children, he only worked in his father's business. When he was picked on by Elijah the prophet, he had to go home and tell his parents that he has been chosen as a son to minister to the prophet.

In those days, when you are a son of a prophet, you are sold out. You were like a slave in a good way. It was a prestigious position. Elisha served Elijah and did not need to take care of any wife or children.

When the husband to this widow became his servant, Elisha didn't understand that this man needed to feed his children and his wife. The man feared the Lord; therefore, he lived his life totally in service to his man of God the prophet.

Would you ask, did he get paid for the services he rendered to his man of God? If perhaps he didn't get paid, was his last resort borrowing to make sure he fed his children and his wife. In the process of borrowing and providing for his family, he was so buried in debt.

Have you also asked yourself what killed a son of a prophet whom the Bible recorded was perfect in the services he rendered to his master the prophet?

Did he live a very stressful life serving the man of God and had nothing in return? Were his needs neglected by the prophet his father? You know, by what I know today, and by the grace to tap into the prophetic and revelational knowledge of the Holy Spirit, I understand that stress and poverty can send a man to an early grave. And I ask again, did Elisha the prophet neglect his servants and sons?

Going back to what I was saying about Gehazi, he knew the woman and he also knew her husband. If you look at Gehazi very well, you will understand that he was knowledgeable. Let me give two instances to prove to you that he was knowledgeable. You remember when the Shunamite woman who had furnished an upper room for Elisha to keep him comfortable whenever he was in town? 2 Kings 4:10-14. Elisha was looking for what to give back in return for the favor, the woman was wealthy, and had connections, so there was nothing in the material world that she could benefit from Elisha, rather she had much to give. Gehazi had knowledge about this woman, he knew the people around. He told his prophet Elisha, there is one thing that the woman lacks, she had no child, and her husband was old. The prophet didn't have that information, as prophetic as Elisha was. He saw deep but didn't know the need of the woman, but Gehazi had that knowledge.

Second instance that made me conclude that Gehazi wasn't a dull person, he may not have been spiritually uptight which could be as a result of poverty and lack of proper coaching by the prophet his master.

You remember that Naaman the Assyrian had gone to the king of Israel with a letter from the king of Syria requesting him to cure Naaman of his leprosy? The king rented his garment apart, and the Bible said when Elisha heard that the king rented his garment, he sent a message to the king requesting him to send Naaman to him. (2 kings 5:1-8).

Now, let me ask you a question, who told Elisha that the king rented his garment? It was Gehazi who gave him that information. Gehazi knew what's up, he knew the peoples whereabouts, and he had privy to information that the prophet didn't have physically. I am by no means saying that the prophet couldn't have decoded this information if he wanted to or if God wanted him to, I am just saying that Gehazi wasn't a dull servant, he provided his master the prophet with information about anything he noticed around the city and country, he was privy to certain level of information.

Another thing to bring to your attention is this, Elisha was very connected, he wasn't in lack, so there was no need for his servant to die leaving a widow and two sons in debt.

Elisha said to the Shunamite woman, do you need me to give you some connections to the government or the military? 2 Kings 4:13. If Elisha didn't have connections, would he had offered one to the Shunamite woman? Then, why would his servant, a man who served him faithfully die hungry and in debt?

Gehazi was also probably having the same issues of providing for his household at the time when he was faced with the greatest temptation of his life. How do I know this? Because it is right there in the Bible. It's hidden, you just have been so focused on the issue that he lacked spiritual judgment to know that he shouldn't have done that.

Let me take you to where you will find the answer. In 2 kings 5:5, when the King of Assyria told the captain Naaman to go to Israel to receive his healing, the Bible recorded that he took some gifts with him. He took Ten talents of silver, six thousand pieces of Gold and ten changes of raiment. Those were what he presented to Elisha the prophet as a thanksgiving offering.

Now, let's go to 2 Kings 5:22, what did Gehazi ask the captain for? He asked him for just one talent of silver and two raiment.

You see, Gehazi didn't ask for gold and lots of money, he just asked for enough money to settle his debts and two garments so he can change his old clothes. Who knows when was the last time he had a change of garment that would make him ask Naaman for two garments?

Okay, do you know how much a talent of silver is worth? It's worth 75 pounds. That's how much Gehazi needed to settle his debt, to keep his family safe from debt.

I know that Naaman gave him much more gifts, but what I know by the Spirit of God was that Gehazi asked for a talent of silver because that's how much he needed to settle his debts, and few change of clothes because he needed to change his old stricken garments.

I conclude this portion by telling you that, there are many servants of the prophets and of other men of God, who have fallen into deep issues because they have been subjected to inhuman treatment by their men of God or Papas as they call them.

It really brought tears to my eyes when the Holy Spirit began to speak to me about this special case referred to as the greed of Gehazi in the Bible.

Many children of God have been abused and neglected, and as a result fallen into despair and into the hands of Satan because of how they have been treated by their papas. And when they make any mistake or fall into any temptation, they are cursed by their men of God or papa.

It will interest you to know that by the Holy Spirit, I was made to understand that the leper that came to Jesus in Mathew 8:1-4. Who pleaded with Jesus saying, "If you are willing, you can heal me and make me clean?" Guess what

Jesus said to him "I am willing, be healed!" The Bible said that instantly, the leprosy disappeared. This healed leper was the generation of Gehazi. You know when Elisha cursed him, he said "...you and your generation will suffer from Naaman's leprosy forever." In other words, this curse Elisha laid on Gehazi was permanent and was generational. No man had the ability to reverse this curse. It was only the man called Jesus that had the ability to wipe that generational disease away from Gehazi's generation.

Hence when the man met Jesus, knelling down before him, he said to him, I know this maybe just a try of my luck, I heard about you, that you are generous and very compassionate. I heard, you are different from other prophets and men of God, I heard how you have touched lives, but my problem is a generational problem that no man is permitted to wipe away. But since you are different, and if you are willing, please take this generational curse away from me. And Jesus did!

Do you know another thing that Jesus did? He told him to take an offering, such as required in the law of Moses ... it will be a public testimony that he has been cleansed." Jesus was basically saying here to take the offering that his forefather Gehazi received that brought the leprosy to them back to the priest. Because the priests were aware that the curse on Gehazi's generation was permanent, and no one was supposed to remove it from them.

But, if the master said so, and the offering that caused them problem was returned to the priest, now it becomes public that Gehazi's generation curse was removed by Jesus.

And just to clear your doubts, Jesus healed many other lepers in the Bible, none did he specifically give an instruction to bring an offering to make it a public testimony about his healing. Elisha cursed Gehazi, and the curse was generational based on the law of Moses, that no priest was able to cleanse them of that curse.

Only Jesus could have taken this generational curse away from them. No man will be able to place a generational curse on you as a child of God but stay away from men who are mean at heart. Men who abuse their priestly and prophetic powers against the children of God.

I am by no means endorsing greed, but if you have a need, speak to your prophet and your man of God, don't be foolish to fall into the hands of Satan.

In other words, your prophet, and your man of God needs to train you properly, to depend on and have a relationship with his God, so that his God may also make you a blessing.

Elisha was a very stingy prophet, and out of all the people that served him, he never released his mantle to anyone, he took his gifts, those deposits from Elijah to the grave.

Jesus As A New Testament Prophet

Jesus before he introduced his disciples into ministry, provided for some of them and their families, as was recorded in the scripture. I know you never thought about this but let us look at the event surrounding the call of Peter, James and John the sons of Zebedee. In Luke 5:1-11, the bible narrated that after Jesus had borrowed Peter's boat to enable him to teach the multitude of people who were hungry to hear from him. After the teaching, Jesus said to Peter to launch into the deep for a catch. Though Peter was hesitant because they had fished all night without a success, but he said, "at thy word I will". They had a great catch that filled two boats, and they beckoned on their partners to come and help. The next thing that happened, they pulled the boats full of fishes and secured it, then left everything to follow Jesus.

This was an example of a great provision from Jesus for these disciples who left all to follow him. From the catch of fishes, worth enough to take care of their families for the period they would be with Jesus. The disciples didn't need to borrow to sustain their families. You remember the case of Judas, the one who betrayed him, he was the financial secretary, who oversaw all the spending.

Another instance was before Jesus ascended to Heaven, after he was resurrected, he went looking for his disciples, and they were already about their businesses. Meaning they still had business on the side. The bible recorded that Jesus met them fishing, and asked them if they caught any fish? They said no, and he told them again to launch into the deep again, and they had another great catch of fishes. John 21:1-19. The fishes they caught was enough to settle their families and their children while they prepared for ministry.

These are examples of Jesus providing for his disciples. If you focus on Jesus and how he lived, you will not treat your sons poorly in ministry.

Our example is Jesus, Paul said follow me as I follow Christ. (1Corinthians 11:1). This has become a dangerous venture today in the kingdom of our Christ. Because when you are following a man of God, and you do not know Christ, how do you know when they are no longer following Christ? The best thing to do this last days, is to follow Christ first before you follow any man of God, because without you focusing on the true image of Christ, you will be deceived by last days false prophets and apostles who do not have any relationship with Christ.

The bible said, "And we ALL, with unveiled face, continually seeing as in a mirror the glory of the Lord, are progressively being transformed into his image… (2 Corinthians 3:18).You should make a continuous effort to focus on the glorious image of Jesus Christ, his character and his life on earth, learning how he did things, you will certainly become like him, and transformed gradually into that very image that you focus on. The problem today in the church of our Lord Jesus Christ is that many are focusing on the images of their men of God, their Papa, and are being transformed into that same image. In other words, whoever image you focus on, you get transformed into. That is why when your man of God falls, you also fall because you don't know the difference.

There are men of God who are champions in the kingdom, and should be emulated, but things are falling apart in the Kingdom today, and to be safe while you revere your man of God, let your focus be on the Image of Jesus Christ, that's how you can be strong and do exploit, and support your man of God rather than weighing him down.

What's in stock for your children and their children?

David said since I was young, and now I am old, I have never seen the righteous forsaken or his seed begging for bread. (Psalm 37:25). What does this mean? The meaning is as simple as you can interpret it to be. The righteous cannot be forsaken, secondly his seed will not beg for bread.

Now, if you are ignorant of this knowledge that whatever you're doing good or bad will also be accounted to your children's account, you continue to live your life the way you do.

Most of the problem we have been facing as a generation is from our fathers. God is so principled that no matter how much he loves you, he cannot break his principles. His principles are in his words and his words he has exalted above his own throne. It then means that, you can be rest assured that the word of God will come true. It's a covenant! You know, Satan covenanted and still covenants with fathers and mothers to buy up the generations of their children. Hence, many who join secret cults, witchcraft and other diabolical activities are so deceived in their selfishness.

It's a selfish thing for you to live the way you do, and not consider the future of your children or the next generation. When you steal public funds, mix manage public money spend money on illegal activities, do you forget that the next generation is at stake?

Consider whether your next step, will be borrowing from your children's account or will be depositing into it? Will you be selling their rights to life, or you will be adding to their lives? Think about your actions and your inactions, how is it affecting the next generation? Will your children beg for bread due to your selfish desires and lusts?

Do you know that, if you have been feeling forsaken, it may be because your parents were ignorant enough, and failed to secure a future for you? Ignorant is never an excuse, they were ignorant enough and that's why you're where you are. Would you like your children to fight the same battles, and struggle more than you have struggled in life? It's up to you, your next actions or quietness can determine what you want for them.

Noah offered on the Altar he built. For the sake of sacrifice, which was well done and cleanly done, God removed the curse he placed on the ground in Genesis 3:17 when Adam sinned. As long as the earth exist, whenever a man sows a seed, he will get a harvest. This would warrant you to know that whatever kind of seed you sow, you will reap a harvest. In Galatians 6:7 Paul said to them, "do not be deceived for God cannot be mocked, whatever a man sows he will reap" He went further to explain that when you sow in the flesh, you shall reap in the flesh (corruption) and he also advised that when you sow in the spirit, you will in due season reap life everlasting.

In Genesis 8:22, God continued to say that there will be seasons such as cold, and heat, and summer and winter, and day and night. In other words, if you are on the earth, you will experience cold, and heat, summer and winter, day and night. And depending on the kind of seed you are sowing; you will also reap a harvest.

CHAPTER TEN

SPIRITUAL BLINDNESS: MYOPIA- NEAR SIGHTEDNESS

As DISCUSSED IN THE PREVIOUS chapter, the reason the prophet of God, Elijah the Tishbite abandoned his servant who did an exploit with him on Mount Carmel, was because the servant suffered a sickness medically known as Myopia: a visual challenge where a person can only see things that are near to him, but once the object is placed further, they lose the visual field to connect properly.

Myopia can also be known as Nearsightedness, and the names are usually used interchangeably. It is an interesting topic, because many people in this generation suffer from this problem; not just physically, but more like spiritually. We are going to consider Prophet Isaiah, Ezekiel, Father Abraham and king Nebuchadnezzars.

In the year King Uzziah died

Isaiah said in Chapter 6:1 "in the year when King Uzziah died, he saw also the LORD..." in other words, King Uzziah had to die for Isaiah the prophet to see the LORD.

Every prophet has king Uzziah. And king Uzziah usually is that person of influence over a prophet. King Uzziah is that person that a prophet seats at meat at his table. It is that person that invites you over, to inquire what God is saying about a matter. And it's not just because he really considers what you have to offer, it is because he wants to confirm if he should go ahead with his heart decisions.

King Uzziah is that man that would ordinarily make you choose your words when delivering a message. King Uzziah is that person that makes a prophet a false prophet, not because the prophet lacks the ability to hear what God is saying, but because the prophet waters down his message to the point that a lying spirit takes over his tongue. King Uzziah must die for a prophet to see the Lord and become a true prophet. In Isaiah's life, king Uzziah was a reason why Isaiah couldn't see the Lord, and thereby suffered from a visual disorder and impediment which deprived him the ability to see God.

And the LORD Said to Abram!

Abram and his nephew started off on a journey from his father's land after God told him to depart for a land he would show him, a land that was flowing with milk and honey. The instruction Abram got strictly said leave his country, his people and his father's house, but Abram took his nephew (his father's house), his servants and his nephew's servants (his people), (Genesis 12:4). In other words, he violated two out of the three instructions given to him. He left his country but took his people and his father's house (Lot his brother's son). Abram was compassionate, he couldn't let his nephew off his sight because, his brother who was his father was already dead. (Genesis 11:28). But God had instructed him to leave everyone, and his country because he knew what would happen when you get someone who lacks the ability to see what you can see. Meaning, when God gives you a vision, bringing a person who does not understand that vision to walk with you is a disaster.

Fast forward into the future when Abram had to separate from his nephew Lot, because his servants strove with Abram's servants. (Genesis 13:5-7) Just to let you know that Lot had this spiritual disease called myopia (nearsightedness), when the disputes arose among their servants, "So Abram said to Lot, "Let's not have any quarreling between you and me, or between your herders and mine, for we are close relatives. Is not the whole land before you? Let's part company. If you go to the left, I'll go to the right; if you go to the right, I'll go to the left." Lot looked around and saw that the whole plain of the Jordan toward Zoar was well watered, like the garden of the LORD, like the land of Egypt. (This was before the LORD destroyed Sodom and Gomorrah.) So, Lot chose for himself the whole plain of the Jordan and set out toward the east. The two men parted company" (Genesis 13:8-11).

Lot could only see what was closer to him, only in the physical, as he examined the land, he saw the land that was well watered, with much vegetations, and he choose that portion of the Land.

As short sighted as he was, he could only see in the natural, he could only see with his physical eyes. If he was spiritually intoned, he would have known that though that land looked well flourished, and had greenish vegetation, there would be a plan to destroy the land and the people who dwelled in it due to their level of atrocities in the future (Sodom and Gomorrah).

Lot was so inconsiderate and selfish, if not, he would at least consider that Abram was his uncle, who was already seventy years old as of this time. He should have said, since you were nice to take me with you Abram, and didn't leave me behind to die, I would rather you choose first, then I take whatever you give to me. But no, short sighted people are usually unwise, and selfish, that's why they lack the ability to judge right.

God, who is the Judge of all, was patiently watching and paying close attention as well. Once Lot was separated from Abram, the LORD God showed up, as if he was desperately waiting for them to part ways. Sometimes, when you don't separate from the location, people and relative that God wants you to sperate from, your vision and purpose in life would be limited or stalled.

Sources of what you see: your visions and dreams

You know as children of God; we see in both the realm of the spirit and physically. In the realm of the spirit, there are two major sources of what we see: Godly visions (positive sources) and demonic dreams (negative sources). Whenever God wants to give you a message, or speak to you, apart from his audible voice, he gives you an image of things, and will either interpret it for you as a message or give you an understanding of the image.

There are multiple examples in the bible, ranging from the prophets to kings, God spoke to and through prophets using visions and images, and he also spoke to kings especially in times of Judgement using images and visions.

Ezekiel, the Prophet (positive sources)

In the valley of the dry bones, God said to prophet Ezekiel after he showed him in the spirit a valley filled with dry bones, "Son of man can these bones live?" Ezekiel 37:3. First I need you to note what happened before the question, Prophet Ezekiel said that the hand of God (the Spirit of God) was upon him, and he was taken in the spiritual realm into a valley, and in this valley, he was also made to walk back and forth, but something happened while he was walking back and forth, he saw images of many dry bones, and these bones were very dry, then God said… Ezekiel 37:1-3

The point I am trying to make here is this, God wanted to communicate with Ezekiel, and he wanted him also to prophesy, but the first thing that had to happen was for Ezekiel to see a clear picture of the message God was trying to give unto him. Without a clear vision or images of what God wanted him to see, he would not have understood the message God was trying to convey to him.

Ezekiel was a prophet of many visions and images, God spoke to him many times with illustrations of images. Some, he would show him an image, then he would tell him what to do. Others he would ask him "do you see this or what do you see?" Ezekiel 47:6, the point here is, God is the number one source of spiritual visions and dream.

King Nebuchadnezzars: (positive sources)

Another example is the story of the dream of king Nebuchadnezzars, in the book of Daniel Chapter 2:1-8. The king had a dream, and he didn't understand that dream, (that is the difference between kings and prophets, the prophets are opened to understanding their visions and dreams, while the kings do not). The king requested that all the magicians, astrologers, sorcerers be brought to tell him the dream, then give him an interpretation. None of them could tell him the dream (because they were not the source of the dream, and do not know or connected to the source either). In fact, they said to him, "There is no one on earth who can do what the king asks! No king, however great and mighty, has ever asked such a thing of any magician or enchanter or astrologer. What the king asks is too difficult. No one can reveal it to the king except the gods, and they do not live among humans" (Daniel 2:10-11). Isn't this very interesting that they said that only the gods could give the king what he was asking for, and these gods do not live among humans. They lied, because Daniel is about to prove them wrong.

As a result of their answer, the king ordered that all the wise men in the land be killed, and Daniel was among the wise men, so he was called to prepare to be killed. But Daniel had a different source and spirit, he was from the Almighty God, and when he heard the news, he went in to ask the king for time so he could inquire of the God that has the matters of man in his hands. It so happened that night that God revealed exactly the image he showed the king to Daniel and gave him the interpretation as well.

When Daniel met with the king, narrated the images and their interpretation to him, the king fell on the floor, and worshipped Daniel, not only that, but he also ordered that offering and incense be burnt before Daniel, (Daniel 2:46). How could Daniel ever imagined that the King that ruled over other kings would fall on his face to worship him, because of his talent? Also, what a God? He was able to show Daniel the exact image then the interpretation of these images. You remember I said earlier, that when God reveal things to prophets, he also gives them the interpretations of the things they see, but to kings, he gives images, then they must look for a prophet to give them the interpretations. This was exactly what happened here, the king saw the images, but didn't understand the meaning.

Negative Sources

Other sources of visions and dreams or revelations apart from the Spirit of God is the demonic sources. The devil has also mastered the function of the human mind, and through occultic and witchcraft means, create dreams and visions and projects it into peoples lives. You know, Jesus said "the thief only comes to steal, kill and to destroy…", (John 10:10). This is because whenever the devil projects dream into anyone's live, it is for the sole purpose of stealing, killing and destroying. The occult and the witchcraft world use evil dreams to manipulate destinies, and pry into people's stars and destinies. They also used evil dreams to project sicknesses, diseases and death into the lives of individuals.

One major example of devilish revelation that changed the course of humanity was the case of the serpent and the woman at the garden called Eden. This encounter started as a normal conversation, and interaction between the serpent and the woman. In other words, when you dabble into demonic activities, you need to know that the devil is full of deceit and is always looking forward to stealing from you.

The bible said: "The serpent was more crafty than any of the wild animals the LORD God had made. He said to the woman, "Did God really say, 'You must not eat from any tree in the garden?"

The woman said to the serpent, "We may eat fruit from the trees in the garden, but God did say, 'You must not eat fruit from the tree that is in the middle of the garden, and you must not touch it, or you will die.'"

"You will not certainly die," the serpent said to the woman. "For God knows that when you eat from it your eyes will be opened, and you will be like gods, knowing good and evil." (Genesis 3:1-5).

The dream happened in Genesis 3: 6 "When the woman saw that the fruit of the tree was for food and pleasing to the eye, and desirable for gaining wisdom, she took some and ate it. She also gave some to her husband, who was with her, and he ate it. Then the eyes of both of them were opened, and they realized they were naked; they sewed fig leaves together and made coverings for themselves"

The woman saw the image the serpent created for her to see and was convinced that the fruit can make one wise, she took one and ate, then gave to her husband. And immediately, their eyes opened, and they saw that they were both naked.

Let me explain a little deeper, their eyes opened to nakedness because the dream he created for them was that of deceit which sole purpose was to steal from them. And the very thing he stole from them was the image of God, which was their covering, their glory. They had a covering which was the Image that protected their nakedness from showing, but because the serpent who represented Satan there was also naked, his body was stripped off him when he sinned. Ezekiel 28:16

The point I am trying to make here is, your level of sightedness has a lot to do with where you end up in life. If you find yourself with a myopic vision, you will always need to see things at a closer look before you can understand them. More so, if you are spiritually myopic, it is a very dangerous thing as a child of God, because it may take you a longer time to have clarity of spiritual matters. Be careful how you see things, above all pray the Holy Spirit to help you if you have a myopic vision, you cannot see far spiritually with this kind of vision. Not because there is nothing to be seen spiritually, but you lack the visual field to capture spiritual visions well.

CHAPTER ELEVEN

WHY SOME CAN'T HEAR GOD

Jesus said in Mathew 8:38 I speak what I have seen with my Father, but you do what you see with your father. Here Jesus speaks of two different fathers; the first Father which is God, and the second father who is the devil. They (Pharisees and scribes) continued to argue with him that Abraham is their father, but Jesus said nah! Abraham is not your father, because if he was your father, you would not be doing the things that you do. You seek to kill me constantly because you are not of Abraham. Jesus went further to say that if God was your father, you would love me because I came from God.

Jesus also said you don't hear the word of God because, you are not of God. And he passed the judgment about them saying; you are of the devil your father, and you fulfill the lusts of the devil your father. What is then the lusts of the devil? Here in Verse 44 of John 8, Jesus said, the devil was a murderer from the beginning, he lies, he speaks of his own because he is a liar and father of it. The devil only comes to kill, to steal and to destroy.

Anytime you watch someone closely and monitor what they do, you can know whose kid they are. By their characteristics, you will know of whose seed they are. The spirit of Antichrist is in them, because that's what they exhibit. You look in a Country where the head of state encourages killings, lies and other activities, what do you make of it? It's that seed of the devil manifesting through them. They know there are of the devil their father, the point is do you know they're of the devil their father. If you do, it will save you so many questions and praying.

Jesus didn't pray for these special breeds from the devil who called themselves the Pharisees or scribes, because Jesus understood what God said in Genesis 3:15 "I will put enmity between you and the woman, between her seed (Jesus) and your seed". Now who is the seed of the devil? Who is the seed of the serpent? They are all over the earth, just like you and me. They have human fleshes but they are not humans.

When you read and understand the scripture, you will understand why certain people act the way they do, even in the church, and why they can't hear from God. The synagogues represented the church in the time of Jesus Christ. There are certain people, even though they appear as humans, but are they really humans? Though they appear to be walking the earth, they are of a different agenda, because they are of a different heritage and must fulfill the works of their father, the devil.

Sometimes, you wonder if these people have a heart, if they even have conscience, but they don't, because there is no place for a true heart to exist in them. Praying for people like this to give their lives to Jesus is like praying for the devil to repent. There is no place in them to accept the good word of God and change. You can now look at certain World leaders and decipher that they are not humans, and they act the way they do because they are of one mission, to fulfill the lusts of the devil their father!

Complacency

This is another reason why many can't hear from God; they are complaisant with their Christian life. Jesus said to Peter, are you sleeping? Couldn't you watch for one hour? Meaning you couldn't pray for a good whole hour? Mark 14:37-38.

And he continued to say, watch and pray that you don't fall into temptation. Meaning, the thing of temptation will surely come, but being watchful and prayerful will prevent you from succumbing to it. Temptation is a way that the enemy tries to intimidate people especially the children of God, but it's also allowed by God to work out spiritual stamina in you. Whatever you don't desire cannot be used to tempt you. Meaning, temptation usually presents when you have desired something of that nature. Your desire for it may be somehow hidden until you are presented with it. That is why the bible said in James 1:14 when you are tempted, it is out of your own desire that you are enticed.

Jesus also said, the Spirit is willing, but the flesh is weak (Mathew 26:41). Meaning that the thing of temptation comes for your earthly desires, your flesh. In your spirit as a child of God, you want to pray, you want to do good deeds, but you find out that your body struggles a lot because your body desires to sleep, eat, rest etc. Therefore, the Bible says that the flesh is in enmity with the spirit, and in constant war with the spirit. But Jesus gives an example a true answer to defeating your body through his own lifestyle. He would usually get up, leave his disciples and go somewhere to pray, usually in the mountains without distractions. It means that you can, get up, leave your bed or your place of comfort to a place where you can pray.

Jesus was telling Peter to pray to avoid falling into temptation. If you want to defeat the weakness of the body, deprive the body of its pleasures. Number one pleasure of the body is food. Yea, starve your body occasionally, especially when you feel weak in the place of prayer. Have you not noticed that when the enemy wants to weaken your spiritual life, he starts feeding you in your dreams? that's the devils' tactics in weakening your body and subjecting your body to affliction. In other words, if you find yourself failing in the place of prayer, fast, limit the amount of food you consume

Have you also noticed that when God wants to start something with you, he will first, start training you in the area of food consumption? If you can't let food go, you will struggle with ministry and spiritual living.

Fasting doesn't Change God, it changes you by strengthening your spiritual body so you can easily flow with God. For God is a Spirit, and they that worship Him, must worship Him in spirit and in truth. (John 4:24). That's what He desires. Give God what He desires and watch Him change your life.

Prayer is the one major way of hearing from God, and defeating temptation, it's in the place of prayer that you can communicate to God, and he will speak to you in return. If you have been struggling with hearing God speak, develop a life of prayer, and learn also to pray the right way. Let the Spirit of God guide you, if you can't pray, you cant's hear from God.

Character

Mathew 5:13; Jesus said, "you are the Salt of the earth: but is the salt have lost his savory, ...it is henceforth good for nothing, but to be cast out, and to be trodden under foot of men"

This is an amazing statement by Jesus, and we really don't understand it very well.

Jesus is saying as a salt of the earth, if you lose your savor, what good are you? What makes salt savory? Isn't it the characteristics it possesses to give taste to food? If you ever eat a meal without salt, you will understand the true meaning of this statement.

The main reason salt is used for food is its characteristic; the savory nature, to give taste to the food. If on the other hand, the tasty nature of salt is no longer there, it's good for nothing, meaning you can as well do without it, eat your food without it.

Same goes with a man without character. If as a salt of the earth, you get to the point where you can no longer satisfy the needs of the people of the earth as a salt, then, you are as good as nothing.

Read that verse again, you will understand why many men of God and the church is being cast out and being trodden under foot. It's just basically because of one thing, they have lost their savory nature.

The generation we are in, need people who are tasteful and savory. There are needs for people who are thirsting after healing, prison breaks, liberty, deliverance, salvation, provision and protections. Look throughout the needs of people around as a church or a man of God, if you are unable to satisfy any of their needs or rather thirsts, then, the earth where you stand may have no need for you.

If you are a man of God, a church or even as individuals, and you have no character that represents the Kingdom of God as Jesus demonstrated in Luke 4:40-41, then you may not be needed in your community, the earth. What am I trying to say? Do your work very well, don't be deceived, go back to a place of prayer and the word, until something is birthed in you, something that is tasteful, that the people around you need, something that will give taste to the earth.

Don't leave your place of prayer and fellowship with God, until you have been made tasteful or savory. Persevere in the place of fellowship with God, genuinely desire the sincere milk of the word of God (1 Peter 2:2). In other words, if you continue to desire God in the place of prayer, and he notices your sincerity, he will show up.

Yes, God does show up, because it's part of who he is as a good Father. Have you ever sorted to see your earthly father, even after you have done something wrong, and knowing how disappointed he was, he still considered to see you? How much more God the Father, will he not show up after your sincere desires to meet with him?

This is what He loves the most, he desires a relationship with you more than you do.

That's why God, would leave heaven and go into Eden to look for Adam, just to have a fellowship with him. Have you wondered why God would come down from his heaven in the cool of the day to look for man?

Find that place, which is still available today in your heart, God is still looking for man in the cool of the day, because that relationship fulfills his desires too as God.

Never lose that place of fellowship with God, this is what gives you character, it is what gives you tastefulness. Desire it, crave it, that's how you become like him. When you can focus on him, his image, you begin to transform into him, meaning you become like him. (2 Corinthians 3:18).

There is a popular story in the Bible where Jacob when he was treated wrongly by his master, his uncle Laban. Jacob wanted to move on with his life, but suddenly his uncle had a negotiation with him. They agreed on that negotiation, but Laban was cunning, he separated all the animals that met Jacob's description of what he wanted as his wage and moved them to his sons and moved them three days apart, so that they wouldn't be able to cross parts.

Jacob as a shrewd man, devised his own means, made rods with speckles and spotted, placed them in the places where the animals would come to drink water; that's where mating took place too. While the animals were in communication and communion with another, they would visualize the speckled and spotted rods in the gutter, and they would produce offspring with those kinds of traits. (Genesis 30-25-43).

And the Lord said to me "Whatever you can visualize in the place of communion, you can give birth to". This is to tell you that in the place of fellowship with God, you will become what you see. If all you see is Jesus and His character, then that's who you will become in the place of communion. Build your character, and make it circle around the need of what God placed you on the earth to become. A character that is not built to conform to the true image of our Lord Jesus Christ will limit your ability to hear from God.

Your Work

Your work shows who you are, it's the display of your character. Mathew 5:16-17

Jesus said, let your light so shine before men, that they may see your work and give glory to your father which is in heaven (Mathew 5:16).

You see when people begin to talk about grace, many mistake it to mean the absence of work. Grace doesn't mean you shouldn't work. Grace means, while you are working, you are guaranteed a success. That's the true meaning of Grace.

You know, when the earth was cursed by God for the sake of man, it became hard for man to have a bountiful harvest without God's help. That God's help is what Grace is. The earth was cursed, and Jesus came to redeem man from the curse. Jesus coming didn't remove the original mandate from God for man to guide and dress the garden which was a form of work God gave man.

Dressing and keeping the garden was the responsibility that God gave to man on the earth. Now after Jesus came to redeem man, he redeemed man back to the original form, dressing and keeping the garden. The garden now is what he called the Kingdom of God. Keep the Kingdom that you have inherited. Therefore, Jesus said, occupy until I return, take care of this kingdom that you entered. Inherit it, and preserve it, so that you don't lose it.

Was the law Abolished?

Jesus went further to say in Mathew 5:17, don't make mistakes in thinking that I came to abolish or destroy the law, he said that his coming was to make the law complete. Meaning, to make sure nothing is missing, and nothing is broken. In Other words, those questions that were raised about the law, the doubts that people had about the law, Jesus came to address them.

Example, the issue of the woman caught in adultery, the law said she should be stoned to death, but Jesus fulfilled this law by saying that the only one who is worthy of stoning this woman to death is one without sin. Though, it is the law given by God, and Jesus being God couldn't contradict himself, but he needed to make that law complete by adding the missing part to it. This missing part was what he wrote on the ground when he stooped down to write on the earth.

Jesus wrote the laws of Moses, so he understood where the people were coming from when they said the woman was to be stoned. Being the law giver, the writer of the law, he stooped down to write the missing part of that law, saying "He who is without sin should cast the first stone" (John 8:7).

Meaning, you can only Judge when your own righteousness is complete (2 Corinthians 10:6).

Jesus who is the one without sin, supposedly the only one who had the right to Judge this very woman, did not judge her. He recused himself from

Judging the woman even though he had every right to judge her. This is where Grace comes to play.

The woman caught in the very act was told by Jesus to go and sin no more. The word sin no more was what Grace gave to her. Meaning, there is something that this woman is supposed to do, to refrain or run away from sin. Grace let her go, but grace told her that the conditions to continue to enjoy grace is refraining from sin. Grace forgives, but grace tells you also that in other to continue enjoying forgiveness, refrain from that very act.

That's what it means to say that your future sins have been covered, it's because, as long as Grace is concerned, you can live without sin. In other words, if you are forgiven, and the condition for your forgiveness is that you refrain from sin or you sin no more, if you decide to go back to sin, you are no longer fulfilling the requirements for grace.

That's why Paul said in Romans 6:1-2, shall we continue in sin so that grace may abound? And he went further to say God forbid! How can we after being dead to sin, continue to live in it.

If you understand Paul properly here, he is saying that the reason you are given grace is because you are already dead to sin. Meaning, with grace, sin is no more, but if you realize that sin is still alive, it only means one thing, you never received grace, or that you have abandoned grace.

Going back to the point I was trying to make earlier; Grace gives you the ability to work. This work you are given ability to do, is the work of righteousness, refraining from sin, this is what it means to go and sin no more.

If you read further the book of Mathew 5:19, Jesus specifically said, if you would break the law or teach people to break the law, you would become least in the Kingdom.

Do you know why? Because Jesus knew that people would take advantage of grace in a wrong way. He said, the law is also important and that's why he has come so that the law can be complete. If the law is complete, then there is proper interpretation of it. Grace provides you with the ability to see what the law is saying, and the ability to do what the law is saying. It's wrong to break the law and to teach people that since Grace is here, they could just live anyhow, Mathew 5:19.

People argue that Jesus did away with the Law, no he didn't, he summed up the law into two categories in the New Testament. In Mathew 22:36-40 a Pharisee in the process of testing Jesus asked him a question, Master, which is the greatest commandment in the Law? And Jesus replied him saying; "'Love the Lord your God with all your heart and with all your soul and with all your mind. This is the first and greatest commandment. And the second is like it: 'Love your neighbor as yourself. All the Law and the Prophets hang on these two commandments."

Jesus knew that by the time you love the Lord with ALL your heart, ALL your soul and ALL your mind, then love your neighbor as yourself, you would have completed the law. No one who loves God with his entire being commits sin. Your level of sinfulness is equivalent to your level of hatred towards God and humanity. You know why? If you have ever loved someone, you would do anything possible not to sin against the person. If the Love of God dwells in you, sin would not be an issue. And if you find yourself in sin, check well, love is far from you. Anyone you love, you must make room for them, that's the true meaning of love. There is no true love without a sacrifice; God so loved the world that he gave his only begotten son, (John 3:16). Jesus was the only begotten son of the Father, but out of his love for the world he created, he gave him up, to gain more sons. If you struggle with giving up your sinful nature away to have God, then your love for Him is questionable. Once you know the truth, you will be free from your bondage. It is possible to live a life free of sin, it is called Grace.

It is worthy of convincing you further, by looking at Jesus final statement in the above scripture; he said, "All the Law and the Prophets hang on these two commandments." If said he did not come to abolish the Law and the Prophets, but to fulfil them, but you believe he abolished the Law (did away with the Law), why then do we still have Prophets all over the earth? The Law and the Prophets live hand in hand. Let me tell you again what Jesus did, He summed up the Law into a value called LOVE. Jesus is saying that if you love the Lord your God, and then Love your neighbor as you love yourself, then the Law is complete in you.

I am not saying by any chance that you should go back to reciting the ten commandments, no! what I am saying is this, Grace has provided you with the ability to live and love God. And by the time you have it in your consciousness to love God with everything in you, there will be no place for sin to exist in you.

In other words, living a life outside grace or a life of sin, will limit how you hear and what you will hear from God. He is a Holy God, and you must be holy to communion with him.

Availability Before God

One major way to get an opportunity and to hear clearly from God is through your availability. You must be available. For God, it's always "who shall I send, who will go for US" Isaiah 6:8.

God is always looking for people to occupy an opportunity or take an opportunity. The problem is that many are not available for God's opportunity.

It's always great to present yourself before God and stand as a waiter for an opportunity.

This is how people have become champions in the Kingdom. It is also through opportunities that you get ranks in the Kingdom. Meaning, once you fulfill an opportunity, then God looks at you and present to you more opportunities. If you look throughout the scripture, God's dealings with man and even angels are mostly based on opportunities, and availabilities.

In 1 Kings 22:20- 23, God had an opportunity available for a man who would be able to convince Ahab to go into war with the Syrians and be killed, and God announced of that opportunity, many provided their availabilities. 1 Kings 22:20, "one said of this manner, and another said on that matter "meaning, there was a deliberation on that matter, and there was like an interview section to find out who was most qualified for that opportunity.

In 1 Kings 22:21, a spirit came up and stood before God and said he would do the Job by becoming a lying spirit in the mouth of Ahab prophets.

And in verse 22, this spirit which stood before the LORD got that opportunity, and an ability was made available for him also. How? God told him, "Thou shall persuade him, and prevail also: go forth and do so" 1 Kings 22:22. God spoke his abilities into this spirit and empowered him to prevail against Ahab. This was why, no matter what was told Ahab by this Genuine Prophet Micaiah, (1 Kings 22: 13-30) he followed the false prophecy, just to fulfill the word of the Lord.

Don't make mistakes, there are times when God will strictly go after a man to present him an opportunity to see if the man can make out an availability. Like in the case of Abram who became Abraham (Genesis 12:1-4). In the case of Gideon (Judges 6:11-16) and many other cases.

In the case of David, it was a matter of an availability. Saul was presented with an opportunity to slay the Giant of Gath called Goliath, but rather than take that opportunity, he ran, and hid himself out of fear. David saw that opportunity, he presented his availability to God, who then gave him that opportunity to become a champion. Goliath wasn't David's giant; he was Saul's giant. And remember this very well, anyone who kills your giant for you, becomes your champion. 1 Kings 22:23-27.

Not only was Saul afraid of this Giant, but he also offered his first daughter and riches as a reward to anyone who would kill his giant, Goliath. It will also interest you to know that Saul was also a giant, he was the tallest in Israel (1 Samuel 10: 23-24). so, he could have been a perfect match for Goliath, but he was a coward, and he ran away from his opportunity.

David presented his availability, then God gave him the opportunity to become the giant slayer, the Champion! Whenever God is not able to find a man to stand in the gap or to take up an opportunity, it makes Him very disappointed, because He will have to do it Himself.

A very big example could be seen in Isaiah 59:1-19 where unjust and terrible atmosphere were seen among the man that God created, not only was there so many injustices on the earth, but what God was furious about was that no man was able to take care of these unjust situations he saw in the earth. "It displeased God that there was no Judge in the Earth, and when He looked to see why there was no justice on the earth, why no one could Judge the earth?", (Isaiah 59:15)

God wondered why there was no one to bring Judgment, but he also wondered why there was no one to intercede, "And He saw that, there was no man, and wondered that there was no intercessor" (Isaiah 59:16).

What did God do then? Isaiah 59:16b-18, explained in detail what God did and would do in a situation where He would have to take up the responsibility as a Father, when man fails in a place of availability, God takes up Fatherhood responsibilities.

Looking at this scripture well, you would understand that there were opportunities presented for a Judge (someone to right the wrong) on the earth. And the second opportunity available was for an intercessor (someone who would stand in the gap) between God and Man.

These two opportunities presented, but there were no availabilities; no one was available for any of the opportunities. In other words, no one was available to hear from God, no prophets, and no one was available to speak to God concerning the people, no intercessor.

Another thing that could happen when God looks for a man to take up the opportunity of being God on the earth is destruction. When God looks for someone to stand in the gap, and he could not find a single man based on his standard, his other option may be destruction.

A perfect example is Moses and the people of Israel, God's anger cannot stand idolatry, and it usually makes God want to wipe away a generation. If you look through the Journey of Moses and the people of Israel, you will understand what a true intercessor does. Moses interceded for the people before God multiple times, that is why God didn't destroy them in the wilderness. (Exodus 33:11-17).

Another example is the case of Sodom and Gomorrah, where Abraham was negotiating (a form of intercession) with God about Sodom and Gomorrah and the people that dwelt in it. He negotiated to the point that he had to give up because the atrocities of the people were so grievous, (Genesis 18: 22-33). Could you imagine that Abraham started negotiating with up to fifty righteous men, then to forty-five, to thirty, twenty and finally to ten. And the Lord continued to say to him, "I will not destroy" the land of Sodom and Gomorrah if I found up to ten righteous men in that city. Could you imagine that in a whole city, there were not up to ten people, which would have made God continue to spare the land. It was a terrible situation, even Abraham gave up from interceding.

Another scripture that really captures the anger of God towards a nation without an intercessor or a Judge is Ezekiel 22:28-31. God pours out anger on people when a situation like this arises where even the prophets have also become liars.

Many times, we are waiting on God, seeking for Him to do something regarding the situation, but on the other hand, he is waiting for someone to present his availability for that opportunity.

Samuel The Prophet

Samuel was a unique Prophet of God, whose word never fell to the ground because the LORD was with him, (1 Samuel 3:19). Samuel's availability before God was presented by his mother Hannah, and though Samuel did not come from the priestly lineage, his mother gave him as a gift to God. His mother made him available for God to use him. You know God was already looking for someone who would succeed Eli the priest, because Eli's sons were written off by God due to their lifestyle. The bible said they were sons of Belial, because they were worthless, undisciplined and did not know the LORD, 1 Samuel 2:12.

One would see such a contradiction between the parenting offered by the Priest Eli, and that of Hannah, Samuel's mother. The former neglected parenting which costed him his priestly lineage, while the latter just made her son available for God.

The LORD started to speak to Samuel at a very tender age, and once he got accustomed to the voice of God, he could hear God clearly, and as a result, his word never fell to the ground. Meaning, everything Samuel spoke was the way he said it, and all his prophecies were verified to be true and authentic.

As a result of his ability to hear God well, courtesy of Eli the priest, who taught him how to identify the voice of God, 1 Samuel 3:8-10. It was Eli the priest who taught Samuel how to respond to the voice of God, which at that time was very scarce.

But that's not where I am going to, I am saying that due to Samuel's ability to hear from the LORD clearly, he avoided many mistakes in Israel, and his word was supreme and was regarded more than the words of other prophets.

One of the major mistake Samuel averted from Israel because of his ability to hear God clearly was in choosing the right king to succeed Saul. Many people read through this portion of the Bible as if it is not a big deal, but it is a big deal, because Samuel could have made a major mistake if he did not have the ability to hear clearly from God.

When he got to Bethlehem, according to the instruction he got from God, Jesse and his sons were consecrated according to the custom of those who would participate in the sacrificial celebration. Not only was Jesse and his sons consecrated, the elders also who were to participate were also consecrated. Where am I going with this? Everyone who was to attend the celebration were consecrated, Jesse, his sons, and the Elders. But none of them who were consecrated got chosen or better said were anointed. 1 Samuel 16:1-13

In other words, everyone who presented themselves to the prophet, some got special attention from him because of the way their physique was structured, but none of them were approved for the anointing according to the LORD.

If Samuel didn't hear God well, he could have chosen the first son of Jesse Eliab, to be the king of Israel, because he looked like Saul; he was tall, heavy set and handsome as well. Those were man's abilities and not God's.

When Samuel got to the sons of Jesse who were consecrated, and present, the LORD said no to all of them, he rejected all of them. You could sense the frustration in Samuel's journey, how he would have wondered if he heard well concerning this journey.

Then, after all the seven sons of Jesse who were certified by Samuel to come to the sacrifice were presented, and the Lord rejected them, he asked Jesse, "are these all the sons you have?" (1 Samuel 16:8-11).

Not only did they send for David, the Shepard boy, they all stood up waiting for him to get there. In other words, he had a standing ovation waiting for him when he got there. Remember that at this point, David had not gone through the consecration in preparation for the sacrifice because he was never thought of by his father that he would be relevant enough to be chosen of the LORD.

In other words, he didn't go through the rituals in preparation for the anointing publicly, but have you ever asked yourself this question, how did the LORD prepare David to become the King over Israel, what were his credentials?

Most times, the people God uses mightily, are trained secretly, it is just the way God has been. Jesus was only twelve years old when he appeared at the temple, then he disappeared from the rather, and then showed up when he was thirty and did mighty works for three years and that was it.

As I was saying, Samuel was discrete in hearing God, and as a result, his words never fell to the ground, and God was able to work with him until his death.

If the Lord hasn't trained you secretly to his own satisfaction, he will not present you to the public. And if you force yourself to the public, you will disgrace yourself. To justify this statement, look at the life of David before his brother Eliab.

David even after he was anointed went back to the wilderness to tender his father's sheep. This is one of the qualities that David possessed that made God seek after him, a man after his own heart.

Meaning, God desired David because of the qualities he possessed. 1 Samuel 13-14. Sometimes people read this scripture wrong or better said, people interpret it wrong. Samuel was the one speaking here, and he said to Saul, that God sought after David, a man after his own heart. Here, what Samuel was saying is, God pursued after David, desired David, because he saw something in David that he (God) truly loved. One of the qualities of David was his ability to protect his father's sheep, and up to the point of giving up all including his life to go after bears, lions who came to take the sheep.

God watched how David kept his father's sheep in the wilderness, and how he treated those sheep, and protected them. And based on those abilities and qualities, God choose him to be a king over his people.

Meaning, if David could keep his father's sheep the way he did, and protect them with his life, what about God's own people? Would he not take care of them better than animals?

This particular action could be seen also when he saw Goliath abusing God's people. He immediately saw an opportunity to protect God's own people. When David was looking at Goliath, he imagined what he did to the bear, and the lion in the wilderness. He saw Goliath as a wild beast, and he studied him very well, and was able to see that the only thing that could bring him down was a stone at his forehead.

When David was sizing up Goliath, he watched him secretly as he mocked the people of God, and realized his forehead was open, before he asked what the reward is to take Goliath down.

Let me tell you what happened here, David went to check on his brothers who were in the war front. His father Jesse had asked him to go check on his brothers and to bring them food. When he got there, it then happened to be when both armies (the Israelites and the philistines' armies) were getting ready for battle. The bible said that David went to the battle line to salute his brothers and to see how they were fairing. On getting there, he saw Goliath came out and displayed his mockery for the people of God. David watched how all the Israel army fled from Goliath when he came out. David also heard the men talking about the king promises, to give rewards to anyone who would kill this giant, and his daughter to whoever kills the man.

After hearing the mockery of the armies of Israel by Goliath, David asked to be clear what the men had said the reward would be. He was not asking because he was initially interested in the reward, he would have still killed Goliath of Gath even without any reward, because the man was a disgrace to the people of God. 1 Samuel 17:25-27.

In other words, David wasn't asking for a reward in other to kill Goliath, the soldiers were talking about rewards, and he heard it, then asked to be clear. You know why? Because he had already made up his mind to go after Goliath, just the way he went after the bears and the lions who came after his father's sheep in the wilderness.

Eliab: David's brother

Have you ever asked yourself why David's most senior brother, the first son of Jesse was so angry with David? Mind you David was his kid brother who was very good at tendering sheep. Eliab, being the first son of the family, and by right would inherit anything coming into the family first before other members of the family.

Do you remember how all the sons of Jesse except David were consecrated to attend the sacrificial ceremony organized by Samuel the prophet? In Israel, David would never have qualified for the throne by election, so that's why his father Jesse didn't bother to invite him to the ceremony.

In other words, Eliab would have been the first to be anointed a king according to the custom of the land. But thank God for a prophet like Samuel who heard clearly from God.

The fury that Eliab had against David his kid brother, and the abusive words he used against David was because of the anger he was nursing against David.

Let me make it clearer here, David was a man that God choose over his brothers to be anointed the king over Israel. But David was not prepared by his father Jesse to be chosen. In other words, Eliab, would have been the first to be notified by his father Jesse that the Lord is interested in making one of his sons a king over Israel. And may have been the first to be prepared and consecrated for the throne. Meaning, he had already seen himself on the throne, and would have mentally been preparing himself to become the king after Saul.

Also, when Eliab presented before Samuel, the bible said that the prophet of God said when he saw Eliab, "Surely the LORD's anointed is before me" 1 Samuel 16:6. Which means, Eliab would have heard this statement made by the prophet.

When Samuel the prophet looked through the sons of Jesse, he heard God say he had rejected all of them (1 Samuel 16:9-12), he requested for David to be brought.

When David came, the LORD said to rise and anoint David, which Samuel did, and the Spirit of the LORD came upon David.

This single act of Samuel in the presence of David's brothers, made Eliab so angry that he carried this anger towards David, and displayed it towards him when he came on that day to check on them in the battlefield.

In other words, Eliab, felt David stole the throne from him, and he had developed that hatred towards David. Look at his reaction when he saw David talking with the men about the reward for killing Goliath, the bible said Eliab burned with anger, he was furious, but that wasn't what got my attention, my attention was drawn to his final statement. The Bible said he said to him "...I know how conceited you are and how wicked your heart is..., (1 Samuel 17:28).

He called David deceitful and wicked at heart, just for coming to check on them? How can a man be called deceitful and wicked if not because to Eliab, he stole his birth right, an access to the throne as the king? This was the last time we heard about him; I am sure that David would have stayed away from him. But there was something the Spirit of God was revealing to me about David and Eliab. He told me that some of the hidden battle fought by David were household battles, which majority came from this his brother Eliab.

The Spirit of God told me that Psalm 109 the Psalm of David was written by king David to Eliab his brother.

David endured through Eliab's abuse and curses, and other wicked deeds of Eliab towards him to a point, then he began to cry unto God for help. Psalm 109 was the resultant of David's suffering from the wickedness of his most older brother Eliab. I am sure that by now, you would know that some of the Psalms of David were prayers he tendered to God in response to his household battles.

Availability is a precursor to hearing from God, and not only would you be available, but you must also learn to discern when God speaks. Once you are available, and accustomed to the voice of God, you will hear him clearly whenever he speaks, and it would avert you from many mistakes that many people make today.

CHAPTER TWELVE

IT IS ALL ABOUT JESUS

ALL THINGS ARE DELIVERED UNTO ME!

Jesus said, "All things have been given to me by my Father. No one knows the Son (Jesus) but the Father". Meaning, those who think they know Jesus or the father, may be wrong. He said also the only one who knows the Father is the Son; the Son reveals who the Father is to those he wills, Luke 10:22.

In Mathew 11:28, he invites you and everyone who is struggling and stressing. He said if you are suffering with heavy loads on you, then you can come to him to receive rest. He said again, take up my yoke (joining) upon you. He is saying, it's of a willingness. You can come to me and join yourself to me and learn from me.

Jesus himself says, come and be my student, come let me teach you the things you don't know about life. He said also, because I am a gentle teacher, I am meek, and lowly at heart. Meaning, I am not like the teachers you are used to. My teaching will provide rest for your soul.

The learning of who Jesus is, will give you knowledge about the father. It is in the process of discovering Jesus that you discover that he is like the father, and that he is in the father. If he is in the father, and you are in him, it means you are also in the father. It is in the process of getting to know Jesus and learning at his feet that you discover that you are like Jesus.

Therefore, as you focus on this image (the characters of Jesus) you are transformed (your character is metamorphosed) into his own image (his character). (2Corinth 3:18). It means one thing, as you focus on the characters of Jesus, which only him can reveal, you become like him, walking in him, and manifesting his personality on the earth.

All things, including the ones you are looking for have been given to Jesus by the Father (ABBA), and you can have All things that you dream of and desire, under one condition, come and join yourself to me says Jesus, be yoked with me, then I can teach you how to get all things. It's a process, but once you have it, you will flourish, and you will never lack anything in the Kingdom of God.

The Name Jesus

The name Jesus messed up Satan's ideas and agenda for a long time up until the death of Jesus of Nazareth. You know, the name Jesus wasn't the name that was prophesied by the prophets, and it is the same reason some of our Jewish brothers rejected Jesus as the Messiah.

The prophecies about Jesus by the prophets of the old, said a virgin shall conceive and bear a son and his name shall be called Immanuel, (Isaiah 7:14).

The birth of Jesus was so monitored by Satan, but what got him confused was the name Jesus. He wasn't expecting that name, he was expecting the name Immanuel, and God disappointed him. You know he was already waiting to cut Jesus off, making sure that man is not redeemed back to the father. Therefore, he continued to ask Jesus, "if you are the son of God" Luke 4:3-9. The proper reason why he asked him that question, and nothing else was because he was confused about the name Jesus.

It is the name Jesus that secured Jesus' ministry on the earth until he completed his mission, if he had the name Immanuel, he would have been cut off before the fulfilment of his ministry on earth.

When Satan confirmed that Jesus was truly the son of God, it took three and half years of Jesus on earth for Satan to know he was truly the son of God, then he instigated the prince of this world to kill him. It was the biggest mistake he ever made; killing Jesus, because Jesus' death was tied to the redemption of man back to God the father.

Alternative to the name of Jesus?

In the book of Act 4:1-23, Peter and John where arrested and put in jail for healing a man that was lame for over 40 years. The people who arrested them were the high priests, the scribes, the captains, and the law makers. They had one question for them "...By what sort of power, or in what name [that is, by what kind of authority], did you do this [healing]?" Act 4:7. The Bible said these high priests were greatly troubled because about 5,000 men believed in Jesus Christ, and the news was spreading all over Jerusalem. They then had to find out what authority Peter and John had in the first place.

But Peter who was under the influence of the Holy Spirit answered and said to them " let it be known and clearly understood by all of you, and by all the people of Israel, that in the name of Jesus Christ the Nazarene, whom you [demanded be] crucified [by the Romans and], whom God raised from the dead—in this name [that is, by the authority and power of Jesus] this man stands here before you in good health" Acts 4:10

Speaking further, Peter made a very interesting statement "And there is salvation in no one else; for there is no other name under heaven that has been given among people by which we must be saved [for God has provided the world no alternative for salvation]." Acts 4:12

Peter said that God has not provided the world any alternative for salvation. It then means that regardless of what you wished or think, salvation is only in one name, the name of Jesus Christ of Nazareth.

When the people heard this, and when they saw that the news was spreading throughout the city, they had a secret meeting in order to come up with an agenda on how to stop the name of Jesus from being preached. "...

they began to confer among themselves, saying, "What are we to do with these men? For the fact that an extraordinary miracle has taken place through them is public knowledge and clear to all the residents of Jerusalem, and we cannot deny it. But to keep it from spreading further among the people and the nation, let us [sternly] warn them not to speak again to anyone in this name. So, they sent for them, and commanded them not to speak [as His representatives] or teach at all in the name of Jesus [using Him as their authority]." Act 4:15-18.

what a conspiracy against the name of Jesus? The point here is, conspiracy against the name of Jesus has always been, and didn't start today. You can attest to it that the name of Jesus is very authoritative and makes the devil very uncomfortable. You could pray with any other name or through any other means, the devil doesn't care, but once you begin to move towards the name of Jesus, every demon around starts to shake.

Unfortunately for the devil and his agents, the name of Jesus is here to stay, and is the name that will continue to make his kingdom tremble. The antichrist is a spirit that has entered the church and all over the world, it is this spirit that arouses men and women and negotiates with them about alternatives to that name Jesus.

You can imagine that it was the high priest (religious persons) that came up with the idea of not speaking to anyone or teaching anyone by this name Jesus. In other words, you can teach or pray in the name of Buddha, Krishna, Mohamed, Queen of heaven, etc., with no issues at all, but the world wants name of Jesus to be avoided at all costs.

It's terrible that even those who profess Jesus have also been deceived into believing that there are other alternatives to the name of Jesus Christ or to the Father. The worst place to be is a place where you would believe is right but end up where you did not expect. Jesus said, "I am the way and the truth and the life. No one comes to the father except through me" (John 14:6).

Don't play ignorance anymore, trying to get to the Father (God) through any other name is idolatry. Idolatry is the same as rebellion, a sin of witchcraft.

The True Light

There is a light that lights every man that enters the earth in form of a newborn. If you were born into this world and you survived labor, delivery, and death (darkness) didn't steal you from the hands of your parents; I have good news for you, the light which is the life in Jesus dwells in you. That you don't know this, doesn't mean it doesn't exist.

In John 1:4 the Bible says "in Him (Jesus) was life, and the life was the light of men. Then in the same John 1:9, it says "...the true light that lights every man that comes into the world. As I said earlier, if you are alive, this light dwells in you. If you don't see it shine yet, it's because something is trying to cover it. When you receive the true knowledge of this light, then ignorance which represents darkness moves away, and your light can shine, the light in you will shine, and darkness will not seize, overshadow or overcome it, John 1:5.

Abide in Me!

Jesus said "If you abide in me, and my words (rhema, revelation) abide in you, ye shall ask what ye will, and it shall be done unto you "(John 15:7). You must learn to abide in Him. But how do you abide (Stay or focus) in him if you don't know him? The first thing here is getting to know him. When the disciples were crossing over to the other side as Jesus commanded them to, the storms of life arose, a great storm the Bible said. While they were struggling in the middle of the Sea, they looked out and saw a man walking towards them. To them (the disciples), it was a complicated problem; not only were they struggling to stay afloat and not get drowned in the middle of the sea, they had to also face a ghost. Jesus sensing their fears from where he was, walking on the sea, called out to them and said to them to be still, be calm, it's the master.

And Peter said, (not so sure it's the master, a doubtful heart) to Jesus, if it's you, bid me to come. And Jesus said "COME"! Then, Peter began to walk on the stormy sea. As Peter remained focused on Jesus, he was walking on the stormy sea, but immediately Peter noticed a bigger wave coming towards him, fear gripped him, and he began to sink. Once he noticed he was sinking, he cried out to Jesus who was so close by, and Jesus quickly reached his hand and grabbed him. Jesus said to him, why did you doubt?

Child of God, stay focused and attach your eyes and your imaginations on Jesus. Even if you see the waves of what is happening out there coming at you, stay focused with your eyes glued on Jesus. As you focus on Him, you are transformed from Glory to Glory.

CHAPTER THIRTEEN

SEEKING GOD

Seek Ye First!

Jesus said "Seek Ye first the Kingdom of God and his righteousness, and all these things shall be added unto you "(Mathew 6:33). This is to tell you that the kingdom of God is a person. John the Baptist preached saying "Repent for the kingdom of God is at hand" (Mathew 3:2). He was referring to the person of Jesus. He was that Kingdom of God that John the Baptist was talking about. Jesus took it further when he said, "the Kingdom of God is neither here nor there, it's within you" (Luke 17:21). He was trying to open their eyes to that revelation of who he was, but they couldn't receive it at that time.

Jesus is saying if you can seek the kingdom of God, you can find him, and when you shall find the kingdom of God, and his righteousness, you will automatically magnet all these other things. You know why? Because your Heavenly Father knows that you have need of all these things (Mathew 6:32).

Seeking God entails many things; humbling yourself and desiring to know him, (The Kingdom). While you are desiring to know him, he will open himself to you. And as you focus on seeking him, you will begin to know who you are. And once you can see his image, you can become like him. This is when you have found the kingdom. Once you find him, his righteousness will manifest in your life, and will magnet everything you need to manifest his image and his likeness on the earth.

In the process of seeking him, many things will fall off your life. In the place of prayer, a place of seeking, you will be transfigured. This transfiguration is a metamorphosis that changes everything about you.

Those things that Paul mentioned in Galatians 5:19-21, that would prevent you from inheriting the kingdom will fall off your life. Paul enumerated that those who live in sexual immorality, impurity and debauchery; idolatry and witchcraft; hatred, discord, jealousy, fits of rage, selfish ambition, dissensions, factions and envy; drunkenness, orgies, and the likes, will not inherit the kingdom of God. What Paul is saying here is not that you will not enter heaven, he is saying that these things listed in Galatians 5:19-21 will cost you the inheritance in Christ Jesus. Hence, many Christians are sick, poor and are void of power.

Stay focused, keep seeking; as your deep calls unto his deep, he will begin to manifest his person to you. And he will show you mighty things that you know not. (Jeremiah 33:3).

Why Seek Ye The Living Among the Dead?

In the book of Luke 24:5, the women who included Mary Magdalene, Joanna, Mary Mother of James and other women who were not mentioned sort after the body of Jesus to anoint him, were shocked to discover that the stone was rolled away, and his body was missing.

Instead, they found Two men who wore shining garments. These men said to the women who were looking for Jesus, "Why do Ye seek the living among the dead?" (Luke 24:5)

This tells you that women are seekers, they know how to search out anything they focus to search. But what is interesting here is the fact that they were seeking the body of Jesus, because they wanted to anoint him. Because of the quality women possess, they are seekers, many have been deceived in this process, and many have been victimized because they desired to see the Lord Jesus Christ.

It's also a very painful thing that many have been deceived by religious leaders in their search for the true God. Many churches today are sepulchers where many go in to seek the Lord and never make it out. Many of them have been lied to, molested, humiliated and many are dead spiritually due to lack of discernment. As you seek God, make a discrete choice to pay attention to the leading of the Holy Spirit. The Master Jesus, said in John 16:13, the Spirit of Truth, will guide you into ALL truth. It means if you are falling victims of open sepulchers as churches, you have been bewitched because you have neglected the guidance of the Holy Spirit. Don't live another day in your life without the guidance of the Holy Spirit, learn to yield unto him.

Entering the Kingdom of God

"It is easier for a Carmel to go through the eye of a needle than for a rich man to enter into the Kingdom of God" Mark 10:25). Entering the kingdom of God for the rich young ruler according to Jesus will mean him selling whatever he had and giving to the poor and carrying his cross to follow Jesus Christ. You know here, people often use this scripture to condemn wealth and riches. That's not what Jesus was doing here.

You remember I said earlier that the kingdom of God is a person, and that's exactly what Jesus represents. Here, Jesus was addressing a self-made population, and the generation who has worked hard and acquired wealth for themselves. He is saying, for them to receive the gospel of the kingdom of God which means denying themselves of everything they know and sitting to learn from Jesus what the true wealth is, will be hard. The young rich ruler, inside of his heart understood there is more to this world than what he had seen or tasted. And out of his sincere soul search for completeness, he asked Jesus what he must do to enter the kingdom of God.

Though, this young ruler had all that wealth could provide for him, and as a ruler, he had empires that he ruled, but still had that void in him for the true completeness which comes from a savior. This young ruler said to Jesus that he has kept the commandments which Jesus mentioned form his youth. He then made a statement that is troubling, "What do I still lack" (Mathew 19:20). Do you know what this means? The young rich ruler was expressing his frustration to Jesus, about his level of incompleteness. He asked Jesus why do I still feel incomplete, even though I have followed the law? He said, from my young age I have followed the law, but there is still a vacuum inside that is yearning for a savior, which he described as eternal life. Even with all his wealth and religion, he still hungered for a savior.

Unfortunately, when Jesus offered him the chance to become one of his disciple which would have been a route to salvation, he rejected it, because his money had a hold on him.

If you are not humble, you cannot seek or worship God, because pride is self-worship. You can't worship two masters at the same time, you can only worship God or yourself, or money. Whenever you notice that you are struggling with true worship to God, check yourself well, you are probably idolizing yourself unknowingly or that your money has a hold on you.

Jesus is saying here that people who are considered, self-sufficient and independent, find it very difficult humbling themselves for the need of another, a master. They have become masters according to their own standards, and do not need to submit to another. Entering the Kingdom of God here, would require that the young rich ruler (master), becomes the ruled, and becomes a follower of Jesus Christ; that is a hard thing to do, according to the worldly standard, but with God "ALL things are possible", Mathew 19:26.

A religious ruler

John 3:1-5

Nicodemus a Jewish ruler approached Jesus at night, why at night? Because, he was a very known religious man, and a Pharisees; those who were believed to be closer to God than anyone due to Abrahamic covenant. He didn't want to be seen by people approaching the radical doctrine Jesus, he decided to secretly seek after Jesus. Why? Nicodemus knew in his heart that, there must be more to what Jesus was preaching than his religious routines. His quest and hunger for more led him to Jesus. While he was still gathering his statement, Jesus perceiving in the Spirit understood why he came, he immediately addressed his quest. Jesus said to him, the answer to your question is to be born again. You cannot see the kingdom of God if you are not born again.

Notice here that, seeing or entering the kingdom of God here doesn't mean dying and going to heaven. The kingdom of God here represents a different realm, a different world totally. It's a world where God rules. It's a world where miracles happen, where the sick are healed, where deliverance take place.

As I have said earlier, I continue to say again and again, Jesus is the Kingdom of God, and as this religious ruler called Nicodemus, purposed in his heart to see Jesus, he got a reply that shocked him; "...Except a man be born again, he cannot see the Kingdom of God" John 3:3. The first requirement to seeing the kingdom of God according to Jesus is being born again.

After you have become born again by confessing with your mouth that Jesus is Lord and believing in your heart that God raised him from the dead, (Romans 10:9), then you can see the kingdom of God. According to Jesus, this is the first requirement to even see the kingdom. To the religious ruler, it means a true believe that Jesus is really from the father, not only that God is with him as he confessed in John 3:2, he needed to also believe in Jesus as the Messiah, and that he is also from God. If this was his position, he ought not to have sought the master secretly, or at night like a thief. That was what Jesus was trying to address here, that was what confused him (Nicodemus), and it made him to marvel.

Jesus also progressed to the second requirement to entering the kingdom of God; as he rightfully said in John 3:5, after you have become born again by confessing Jesus as Lord and savior, you can then enter the kingdom of God by being born of Water (Baptism), and of the Spirit (Holy Spirit). In other words, once you see the kingdom, you then need to enter by baptism and by the Holy Spirit (fire).

That was exactly what happened to the disciples of Jesus Christ on Pentecost, they entered the Kingdom of God by the baptism of fire. They were with Jesus, they believed in Jesus, so they saw the kingdom, and in other for them to properly enter the kingdom of God, which is Jesus Christ, they were asked to wait for the Holy Spirit to come; it is the Holy Spirit who leads one into the kingdom of God. It means, without the Holy Spirit, you cannot enter the kingdom of God.

Therefore, Jesus said to them (the Pharisees) when they asked him when to look out for the kingdom; he said to them, "The Kingdom of God is within you "(Luke 17:21) The Kingdom of God is a system and a government where God is the sovereign ruler. Jesus taught his disciples to pray that God's kingdom come on earth as it is in heaven, because, when His kingdom comes, there is peace, there's healing, there's provisions and even when you are surrounded by enemies, you are untouchable.

What am I trying to say? You may have been born into religion and grew up in religion, but religion cannot save you, and you cannot experience God's divine presence or his purpose for your life if you are not in his kingdom. Many have been deceived by religion, the things they practice, are stealing the benefits of the kingdom from them. Their health is stolen, their resources stolen by the same religion, because Satan hides behind religion to keep people bound. Now, I say to you, in this time of perilous exposures to wickedness, please don't allow religion to prevent you from attaining hope which is in Christ Jesus

The freedom you seek is only in Jesus Christ, not in any man or religion, seek to know that Jesus, that no man can give you. Seek to know Jesus the Messiah, not the ones people have preached to you. Choose Jesus Christ as Your Lord and Savior. Ask Jesus to come into your heart and give you an experience that no man would ever give you. Choose to dwell and experience the Kingdom of God.

The Heart

"Is deceitful above all things, and desperately wicked: who can know it" (Jeremiah 17:9)

This was God talking to Jeremiah the prophet. It then tells you that, you don't know people by who they are physically, but know them by their hearts. The heart is where the issues of life reside; meaning if you really want to determine any issue as pertaining to life, check the heart of the individual.

It is the heart of an individual that yearns or cries out to God for salvation first before he can confess it, for it is out of the abundance of your heart that your mouth will open to speak, (Luke 6:45). Meaning, the majority of what you say out of your mouth has been conceived first in your heart.

Jesus would always respond to the Pharisees based on their thoughts, and what is in their heart. Sometimes the Pharisees or the scribes would say something in their hearts and Jesus would respond to them not based on their words but based on the thoughts of their hearts (Mathew 9:4), (Luke 5:22). It is in your heart you can think evil, it is also in your heart you can think good, everything you see in manifestation are the proceeds of the heart.

The best way to know a person is knowing his or her heart. This is how God choose people, based on their hearts. (1 Samuel 16:7). Pray that the Lord would give you the eyes to know people from their hearts, not outwardly; you will never be taken unawares, and you will not go into the wrong business. Go deeper, seek God with all your heart, and you will become like Him when He opens to you.

Blessed are the pure in heart!

For they shall see God, (Mathew 5:8).

The word pure here is a Greek word for Katharos which means free from admixture, or without blemish. Purity is a state of a heart where God manifest to you, and you get God's attention.

Solomon advises in the book of Proverbs 4:23 that above everything else you do, guide your heart diligently. He is saying that it should be the highest priority in your life. Guiding your heart will protect your life. He said that every issue of life, every spring of life comes from your heart.

It is from the heart that wickedness proceeds, it is also from the heart that love, kindness and every other good attribute proceed.

Back to Mathew 5:8, do you want to see God? You must purify your heart. To guide and purify your heart, you must learn how to select your thoughts, you can select what goes through your heart. You can choose what you allow to ponder on and what you delete off from your mind.

Hatred starts in form of thoughts, likewise jealousy and their elder sister envy. These three-give birth to witchcraft which is an act of uncontrolled work of the flesh.

Part of the benefit of having a pure heart is answered prayers. God cannot stand sin, your state of heart will either qualify you to ask from God or cause you to run from God. Man is the one who hides from God. (Genesis 3:8). The devil knows how to make you run from God, he is the accuser of the brethren, but no longer does he accuse man in the presence of God because Jesus has taken that place from him. What he does now is to accuse you directly, he accuses you to your face, and accuses you before other brethren. He will give you hundred thousand reasons why you shouldn't approach God; he will tell you ugly things about yourself and give you reasons why you are better off dead than alive, because he is ugly and wicked.

Second way of guiding and purifying your heart is by controlling what you see, for it's the gateway to your heart. Your eyes are like a monitor that goes through your heart, you can control what goes into your heart by shutting off the monitor like you switch off the TV monitor. Ask the Holy Spirit to help you, the grace is available to them that believe.

CHAPTER FOURTEEN

THE HOLY SPIRIT

In the Spirit

Paul said I pray with my spirit, and I also pray with my understanding. (1 Corinthians 14:15). God is a Spirit and you as a man created by God is a spirit dwelling in a physical body called the flesh. Jesus said, for you to relate to God or worship God properly, you must do that in the spirit and in truth. (John 4:24).

How do you know that your prayer or worship is effective, if it's not done in the spirit? I must open your eyes or perhaps open your understanding to this scripture in 1 Corinthians 2: 14, it says who knows the things of a man, except the spirit of the man in him...? The spirit inside of you which is the true you knows the things that you need. Your spirit knows when you are going to get hurt or can sense if something is going to go wrong. Some people who are a bit sensitive, may sometimes feel an urge to cancel a journey or just stay home for a day because their spirit is restless about their journey.

Your spirit picks up matters from the spiritual realm and tries to communicate to your natural self, but if you are insensitive, you will miss it. Many people are falling victims of their own ignorance, for this very reason. God said in Hosea 4: 6 "my people are destroyed for lack of knowledge" what you don't know is what destroys you.

When you dream certain dreams, it's a way of communication from your spirit of what is ahead. That's why it's important you remember your dreams. God may be trying to reach you, especially if you are not available to hear from God through other channels, because you are a spirit being living in a body. Pray more in the spirit, that's how to align yourself to God; He is a Spirit and must be reached by spirits.

The wind blows

John 3:8

So, it is like to be born of the Spirit, you hear the sounds, you don't know where it's coming from, or where it's going to. To be born of the Holy Spirit, you must be like the wind, people should not see your natural self; meaning you die to yourself. The wind cannot be seen, you die to your own abilities, your ideas, your intellectual desires or reasoning. The wind, which is significant of the Holy Spirit, carries you to anywhere he wills. Submitting to the Holy Spirit is like submitting to the wind, you don't tell the wind where to take you to, he carries you to where he wills. As many as are led by the Spirit of God, they are the sons of God, let God be the leader by His Spirit, Rom 8:14.

How do you Quench the Holy Spirit?

Have you not heard, quench not the Holy Spirit? The book of 1 Thessalonians 5: 19-22 highlights the things you do that can Quench the Holy Spirit. We are going to investigate those things that when you do them, can quench the Holy Spirit.

1. Do not despise prophesyings- do you know what this means? I used to think it means <u>you</u> should not despise when people prophesy to you. But the Spirit of God opened my eyes one day and told me the meaning. The word says despise not prophesying, meaning when you feel the fire in your belly to prophesy, do not quench the Spirit by holding back what he wants to speak through you.

Do not despise the word he is laying in your heart to speak to people or to speak to yourself. Sometimes, you may feel the urge to pray and prophesy to yourself, do not quench the Holy Spirit by ignoring those urges. Sometimes as you pray in tongues, you start speaking mysteries to yourself, prophesying according to God's purpose for your life. If you look at that verse very well, you will understand that quenching the Holy Spirit is an action that only you can perform. Paul could not have been saying to you "despise not" what others are saying to you, he typically is saying you should not ignore when the Holy Spirit wants to use your voice or your person, despising his leading shuts him down.

Just imagine when someone is speaking to you and continues to speak, but you ignore him, at a point he is going to just shut up and not say a word to you anymore. This is what you do to the Holy Spirit when you ignore his leads in your life.

Paul said in 1 Corinthians 14:5 that he wished that all the believers in the church of Corinth spoke in tongues, but his most desire is for all of them to prophesy because he that prophesy is greater than he who speaks in tongue. You can quench the Holy Spirit by holding back what he is saying to you.

2.   Another way not to quench the Holy Spirit is by proving all things. When you go by what you see and what you hear, and forgo a confirmation from the Holy Spirit, you quench the Holy Spirit. Not proving all things means you purposely neglect the presence of the Holy Spirit in your life. Remember Jesus said in John 16:13 that when the Holy Spirit shall come, He shall guide us through ALL truth. Therefore, when you don't recognize the presence of the Holy Spirit by not Proving ALL things as Apostle Paul said, you will Quench Him. He wants to lead, and He wants to guide you through life, and as you go by, doing your own things, you neglect him, and you quench him in your life.

If Jesus said that the Holy Spirit will guide you into ALL truth, and not some of the truth, and he will show you things to come, (John 16:13). Why are you neglecting the Holy Spirit then? His presence can save you a lot of heart aches and give you peace.

The second part of 1 Thessalonians 5:21, says to "prove all things, hold fast that which is good". It means even after you have proved ALL things, there are some things that you are going to see as bad, those one which are bad, throw them away, and hold tightly to that which is good., by doing this, you give the Holy Spirit a chance to manifest in your life.

3. The final thing that Apostle Paul said that could quench the Holy Spirit is appearances of evil, 1Thessalonians 5:22. He said abstain, meaning run away from ALL appearances of evil. That is to say that anything that looks like evil is evil and you should run away from it, so that you don't quench the Holy Spirit.

Grieve Not the Holy Spirit

Grieving the Holy Spirit is different from quenching the Holy Spirit. The Holy Spirit is a person and can be angered or grieved. "And do not grieve the Holy Spirit of God, with whom you were sealed for the day of redemption. Get rid of all bitterness, rage and anger, brawling and slander, along with every form of malice", (Ephesians 4:30-31).

The word "Grieve" here is a Greek word "Lupeo" which is pronounced as "Loo-peh-o". it is the same word for distress, pain, vex. Apostle Paul is saying that the same way you can vex, pain or cause a friend to be distressed, is the same way you can cause the Holy Spirit to be pained, vexed and be distressed. This scripture tells you that the Holy Spirit is a person who has feelings and emotions as your regular friend. You know very well what happens when you make a friend feel pained or vexed, he will withdraw from you. This is exactly what happens when you grieve the Holy Spirit, he withdraws from you.

Paul is saying in Ephesians 4:31, to avoid grieving the Holy Spirit, you need to get rid of all form of bitterness, rage, anger, yelling, slander and every form of malice. It then means that when these things are evident in your life, the

Holy Spirit feel stressed. These things cannot cohabit with the Holy Spirit in your life, it is either you are full of anger, rage, bitterness, slander and malice or you are full of the Holy Spirit.

The Holy Spirit cannot thrive in any atmosphere that is corrupted or tainted by sin. That is why Paul went further to tell us that while we can avoid grieving the Holy Spirit, there are things to do to make the Holy Spirit thrive in us, such as "Being kind to one another, compassionate, forgiving one another…" (Ephesian 4:32).

The ability to sustain the presence of the Holy Spirit in your life is paramount to your own survival as a child of God. To sustain the anointing is like sustaining the presence of the Holy Spirit. And to sustain the presence of the Holy Spirit, you must sustain the environment that he can thrive in. You must learn to acknowledge him and respect him as a person, you must appreciate his person and not neglect him. When you feel his presence, you must give him attention that he needs, get into conversation with him and map out time also to communion with him as a person. That is what it means to fellowship with the Holy Spirit (2 Corinthians 13:14).

Jesus would routinely withdraw from the crowd and from his disciples to a place of prayer, a mountain where he had communion with the Father and the Holy Spirit. Jesus did these things more than he preached the gospel, because his communion with the Father and the Holy Spirit was the secret to his success in ministry. To succeed in life, whether in business, carrier or ministry, you must have a good relationship with the Holy Spirit. Without this, your success has no guarantee.

CONCLUSION

The God of your man of God, can also become your God, only if you are willing. You can experience and encounter the same God your man of God encountered while still under your man of God. The problem is that many feel that God can be monopolized, no man has that ability to own God to himself.

That's why many are holding onto their talents and gifts thinking that they will become less if they share their gifts. That's exactly what happened to John the Baptist, when he thought by announcing Jesus Christ as the Lamb, he is going to lose all his members (disciples) to Jesus and then lose popularity, he then started preaching a different gospel.

Don't forget why Jesus gave the illustration about the kingdom of God and the distribution of talents. Where a man travelling to a far country, called his servants and gave them talents. One of the servants, took his own talent and hid it, making excuses about his master.

First, how do you think that your talent will earn more talents if you don't put it to work? Looking at Luke 19:13-27, when the Noble master returned from his journey, he called his servants to find out what they did with their talents. The first one returned the talents with ten more talents and was given ten cities to rule over. The same as the one with five talents. But the one who was given only one talent, took it, and hid it.

The first point here is, this servant was only given one talent, the noble master understood that he was complaisant and had problem with the understanding of how the kingdom operates, not withstanding, he still extended that grace to him. No one in the Kingdom of God is without grace for something, find where your grace is located and put it to work.

Some have received grace from God, not because they deserve it, but God wants to give them an opportunity, to see what they would do with it. Many have taken their talents and placed it somewhere, because they think either that it is not worth anything, or that it is inferior to what others have.

Now, look at that illustration very well, you will see what happened to those who decided to use their talents, they gained double their talents, and were given cities to rule over. That is exactly how God treat his people in the kingdom, those who exercise their talents, end up gaining more talents. Not just that, they are also given cities to rule; they are made master's over cities.

So, when you see a man of God who is never willing to put his talents and invest in others, they end of losing out. Many don't know that the best way to double one's talents is by investing it into others. Invest in others, and your work will be very easy.

This is what is happening to many today, either hording their talents or doing buying and selling with it. These are Perilous times, and the very elects are almost being deceived. You are to work out your salvation with fear and trembling as Paul said in Philippians 2:12.

Jesus concluded his messages to the Church in Revelation 3:21 by saying, "To him that overcomes will I grant to sit with me in my throne, …as I also overcame…"

If Jesus said, there are some overcoming that you need to do, just like he did and is now seated on the throne with the Father, why are you still very confused? It is a very clear statement, according to Jesus if you overcome like I did, you will also be glorified like I am by my Father.

Do you think that Jesus did all the overcoming for you, and nothing else must be done, why is he then saying to him that overcomes? (Revelation 3:21). You received Jesus, and you entered the Kingdom of God. To progress into the discoveries of the kingdom, you must learn to walk in him (the kingdom that you entered).

Apostle Paul said in Colossian 2:6 "As you have received Christ Jesus the Lord, walk also in him" what does this mean? It means exactly what it says, as you have entered Jesus Christ, which is the Kingdom of God, take a complete walk in him, make it a daily objective to walk in him, to be led of the Holy Spirit.

Paul said also, you should take root and be built up and be established in the faith, being conscious and mindful of what you are hearing and what you are being taught. Making sure you are not deceived through worldly, and traditions of man, which have nothing to do with Christ. He concluded by saying in Colossians 2:10 "You are Complete in Him, which is the head of ALL principality and Power".

Child of God, how do you read this scripture? It is your standing COMPLETE that is the head of ALL principality and power. Do you know that when you stand complete in Christ Jesus, you are the head of all principality and power? Yes! it is in your standing complete in Christ, that manifests as the head of all principality and power.

The church of Jesus Christ needs to take her place, the church which signifies you and I need to stand complete; if the church can stand complete, Christ can return, the church needs to overcome, this is what Jesus is waiting for, there is a desperate need for a great harvest.

Just as Jesus said to the Church of Revelation, I am saying also to you the church of today, if you have an ear, hear well, hear what the Spirit is saying to you today! Revelation 3:22.

Be mindful of what you hear!

SHALOM!

Printed in the United States
by Baker & Taylor Publisher Services